HOWARD BECKER
ON EDUCATION

MODERN EDUCATIONAL THOUGHT
Series Editor: Professor Andy Hargreaves,
            Ontario Institute for Studies in Education

This important series contains some of the very best of modern educational thought that will stimulate interest and controversy among teachers and educationalists alike.

It brings together writers of distinction and originality within educational studies who have made significant contributions to policy and practice. The writers are all scholars of international standing who are recognized authorities in their own particular field and who are still actively researching and advancing knowledge in that field.

The series represents some of their best and more distinctive writing as a set of provocative, interrelated essays addressing a specific theme of contemporary importance. A unique feature of the series is that each collection includes a critical introduction to the author's work written by another influential figure in the field.

Current titles:

Sandra Acker: *Gendered Education*
Robert G. Burgess: *Howard Becker on Education*
Roger Dale: *The State and Education Policy*
Michael G. Fullan: *Successful School Improvement*
Jane Gaskell: *Gender Matters from School to Work*
Ivor F. Goodson: *Studying Curriculum*
Andy Hargreaves: *Curriculum and Assessment Reform*
Martyn Hammersley: *Classroom Ethnography*
Jean Rudduck: *Innovation and Change*
Barry Troyna: *Racism and Education*

Howard Becker
On Education

Edited by
ROBERT G. BURGESS

OPEN UNIVERSITY PRESS
Buckingham · Philadelphia

Open University Press
Celtic Court
22 Ballmoor
Buckingham
MK18 1XW

and
1900 Frost Road, Suite 101
Bristol, PA 19007, USA

First Published 1995

A catalogue record of this book is available from the British Library

ISBN 0 335 19090 1 (pb)   0 335 19091 X (hb)

Library of Congress Cataloging-in-Publication Data
Becker, Howard Paul.
    Howard Becker on education / edited by Robert G. Burgess.
        p.   cm. — (Modern educational thought)
    Includes bibliographical references and index.
    ISBN 0-335-19090-1 (pb).   ISBN 0-335-19091-X (hb)
    1. Educational sociology.   I. Burgess, Robert G.   II. Title.
III. Series.
LC189.B393 1995
370.19—dc20   95-5372

Typeset by Dorwyn Ltd, Rowlands Castle, Hants
Printed in Great Britain by St Edmundsbury Press,
Bury St Edmunds, Suffolk

Contents

Contents

Preface

Ethnographic studies of educational institutions now have an established place within the sociology of education in Britain and the USA. Many studies by major researchers and research teams indicate the intellectual origins of their projects and the ways in which both projects and researchers are indebted to the pioneering work of Howard Becker. Yet there is no single volume containing Becker's work on education to which researchers can turn. Instead, reference is made to a range of papers that have been published in numerous journals and collections of essays over the last 40 years.

This book attempts to bring together some of Howard Becker's writing on education. There are numerous articles that could have been used, but those that have been included convey some of the major areas of Howard Becker's work. In Part 1, we begin with an overview of work on schools in which key issues and problems are identified before turning to a study of the teacher–pupil relationship. In Part 2, we include two classic accounts on teachers and teaching based on Becker's study of teachers in Chicago. In Part 3, we turn to studies of socialization as Howard Becker has contributed much to our conceptual development from his work in this area. We begin with an overview which examines the contribution of the interactionist tradition to the study of socialization, while the second essay in this section includes a discussion of 'situational adjustment' – a concept that many writers have used in ethnographic studies in education. In Part 4, we turn to two reflective essays on studies of schooling. We begin with an essay in which Howard Becker reviews key issues that he and others have identified in ethnographic studies of schools and higher education institutions. Finally, there is an essay on the conduct of ethnographic studies and the problems associated with them.

All together, these essays highlight some of the key issues in Howard Becker's work which focus on the intellectual problems he has identified in studies of schools and higher education institutions, the theories and conceptual schemes he has developed and used as well as the methodological issues that are covered in his work and the work of many others. Overall, it is hoped that this collection of Howard Becker's work will remind ethnographers in education of the significance of his studies.

Robert G. Burgess
University of Warwick

Acknowledgements

Chapter 1: Originally published in *Phylon* (1955), pp. 159–70.

Chapter 2: Originally published in the *Journal of Educational Sociology* (1952), 25: 451–65.

Chapter 3: Originally published in the *Journal of Educational Sociology* (1953), 27: 128–41.

Chapter 4: Originally published in the *American Journal of Sociology* (1952), 57: 470–7.

Chapter 5: 'The Self and Adult Socialization' from *The Study of Personality: An Interdisciplinary Appraisal* by Edward Norbeck, Douglass Price-Williams and William M. McCord, copyright © 1968 by Holt, Rinehart and Winston, Inc., reprinted by permission of the publisher.

Chapter 6: Originally published in *Sociometry* (1964), 27: 40–53.

Chapter 7: Howard Becker, 'A School is a Lousy Place to Learn Anything', *American Behavioral Scientist* (1972), pp. 85–105, copyright ©1972 by Sage Publications, Inc. Reprinted by permission of Sage Publications, Inc.

Chapter 8: Reproduced by permission of the American Anthropological Association from *Anthropology and Education Quarterly* 14:2, Summer 1983. Not for sale or further reproduction.

Chapters 2, 3, 4 and 6 are reprinted by permission of Howard Becker.

Finally, I am indebted to Su Powell for the care and attention she has given to producing this manuscript for publication.

Critical Introduction: Problems, Theories and Methods in the Work of Howard Becker

ROBERT G. BURGESS

For over forty years, Howard Becker has made a major contribution to the study of sociology. Generations of students are familiar with his work on social problems, especially in the field of deviance. His collection of essays entitled *The Outsiders* (Becker, 1963) has been a key work that many students of sociology have had to study, as have generations of researchers. It offers a different perspective to studies of crime and deviance by taking an 'underdog' perspective, perceiving social life from the deviant's perspective. This work has been of such significance that Becker's major contribution to sociology is often located in the sociology of deviance. Yet this is far too narrow, as Howard Becker's work is placed on a much broader canvas. He has made contributions to the study of symbolic interactionism, to the conduct and analysis of social research methodology, especially ethnography (Becker, 1970), and to studies of education, medical education and higher education, art, as well as craft, photography and cultural studies (Becker, 1983; Denzin, 1992). Howard Becker has contributed to a range of different fields and sub-fields in sociology.

Among the first area to which Becker turned his attention was the study of schools and teachers. This formed the basis of his PhD thesis at the University of Chicago in the early 1950s (Becker, 1951b). The result was a series of articles on schools and schooling that have influenced generations of researchers in the interactionist and ethnographic traditions in Britain and the USA. Subsequently, Becker also worked with a number of colleagues in research teams where aspects of interactionism were applied to studies of medical education, and higher education (Becker *et al.*, 1961, 1968). Howard Becker's work is the product of wide-ranging interests in symbolic interactionism and research methodology. Indeed, his theoretical and methodological studies have resulted in a range of insights about the social processes that occur in various areas of social life including education.

This introduction locates the work of Howard Becker within sociology before examining some of the general issues raised by his papers on education, as the sociological problems he has investigated are directly influenced by his theoretical and methodological interests. We begin by locating Becker's work in sociological theory and the way in which this has influenced the choice of problems that he has studied, and the methods by which he has chosen to study them. Finally, we examine some of the conceptual insights that he has provided in his studies of educational settings, his influence on the work of other researchers and the extent to which he has provided an enduring research agenda.

Locating the work of Howard Becker

Within much of his work, Becker locates himself within the sociological tradition and in turn within the broad category of a theory based on the concept of symbolic interaction which is found in the work of Dewey, Cooley, Mead, Park and others. Symbolic interactionism involves a range of approaches and traditions, but is often considered to include the work of sociologists and social psychologists based in the University of Chicago. The first generation of interactionist work is generally considered to have been developed by George Herbert Mead, William James, William Thomas, Charles Cooley and Robert Park, who in turn were followed by a second generation of writers including Herbert Blumer and Everett Hughes, and then by a third generation of scholars including Howard Becker, Anselm Strauss and Erving Goffman (Rock, 1979; Denzin, 1992). Among the writing from these groups, it is the work of Herbert Blumer that is most frequently cited for an outline of assumptions on which symbolic interactionism is based. First, it is argued that 'human beings act towards things on the basis of meanings that things have for them' (Blumer, 1969, p. 2). Secondly, the importance attached to the way in which meanings arise out of social interaction is stressed and finally, that meanings are modified on the basis of interpretation by individuals interacting with each other.

While Blumer has been an important exponent of this tradition (Hammersley, 1989), he has also been responsible for mounting a major critique of interactionism through his analysis of *The Polish Peasant* that was published in 1920 by Thomas and Znaniecki. Blumer's summary of methodological and theoretical criticisms not only relate to *The Polish Peasant*, but also more generally to interactionism, as he raised concerns about the quality of data used to test a theory, the use and analysis of documentary evidence, the position of the researcher within research, the definition of terms and the role of theory in relation to research evidence (Blumer, 1939). Similar criticisms were also raised by Manford Kuhn (1964) who argued that testable generalizations could not be obtained from such work – a criticism linked with the theoretical and methodological development of symbolic interactionism.

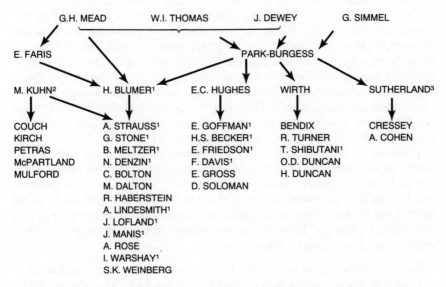

Figure 1   Writers involved in the development of symbolic interactionism

Notes:
1. Interviewed by Jef Verhoeven.
2. The group working with Manford Kuhn are known as the Iowa School.
3. The Sutherland group were not part of the Chicago tradition but were influenced by Mead.

Source: Verhoeven (1989), p. 14

But we might ask: How did Howard Becker become involved with this tradition of sociological work? This issue has been explored by Jef Verhoeven (1989) when he examined the sociological influences upon a range of writers associated with the symbolic interactionist tradition. To conduct his study, Verhoeven interviewed individuals who worked within this tradition and who graduated in Chicago between 1945 and 1952, having worked with Herbert Blumer. He locates many of those in the Chicago interactionist tradition by charting intellectual relationships between different writers during the immediate Second World War period.

The people who Verhoeven interviewed for his study are shown in Figure 1 which provides a guide to those writers working within the symbolic interactionist tradition and the links between different groups within the Chicago School as well as members of the Iowa School who were associated with Manford Kuhn, an advocate of a valid, testable and empirical symbolic interactionist theory. In broad terms, the links between the different groups are similar to those identified by Denzin (1992), who suggests a series of key phases in the development of symbolic interactionism over the last hundred years: the canonical phase (1890–1932) which he links with the work of Dewey,

James, Mead and Peirce, together with such work as Thomas and Znaniecki's *The Polish Peasant* (1918–20); an empirical/theoretical period (1933–50) represented by the work of Mead and Blumer; and a third generation of studies within the period 1951–62 when new texts were produced that radically changed the work of interactionists. It is this phase to which Howard Becker belongs, building on the work of Everett Hughes and Anselm Strauss through a model of identity change as well as developing the use of participant observation. These developments occurred through studies of educational organizations, organizational careers, and personal change through adult life. As Denzin and Verhoeven demonstrate, Howard Becker belongs to that group of sociologists who are linked to the Chicago School tradition.

It was in the University of Chicago Department of Sociology that Becker registered for the degree of MA and subsequently wrote his PhD thesis on the role and career of public school teachers (Becker, 1951b). His thesis Director was Everett Hughes, but Becker recognized that his work was also influenced by Herbert Blumer when he discussed the interactionist tradition in an interview with Verhoeven. Here, Becker provides an outline of the major influences on his work when he states:

> So Herb [Blumer] was not on my dissertation committee, but everything I learned in that general theoretical way I learned from him. He didn't get on personally, he wasn't personally very close to Hughes. I never understood exactly what that was about. I assumed, I was enough of a Freudian to assume that this was sibling rivalry. Both children of Robert E. Park. And I think there was a lot of rivalry in that generation of people as to who was really the heir of Robert Park. And in fact, each one of them represented a different aspect of Park's thinking, it's quite interesting. You know Blumer there, is that general theoretical cast to Park's thinking. And then there is all that interest in all these wild, wonderful details which Everett [Hughes] represented. And so on. So there were people around there including Blumer, who had a big impact on everybody, even though they were not on your dissertation committee. I think looking back, for instance, that Robert Redfield had an impact on me. I took a class from him, but I was never close to him, but he was around there and this thinking was everywhere. The main people who influenced me were Hughes who was the director of my thesis, uhh . . . Blumer and Lloyd Warner, who uhh . . . that was a distinction that some of the people who studied with Blumer and Hughes had very little to do with Warner. I did, Friedson did, Erving Goffman did.
>
> (Verhoeven, 1989, p. 25)

Such comments provide us with an insight into the life and work of the Chicago Department of Sociology where disputes occurred between different writers within the interactionist tradition and where doctoral candidates had to decide what links to forge and allegiances to make. For example, Herbert Blumer saw society as an on-going process in which participants were involved in joint interactions – a situation which was rooted in a career that was fixed and full of uncertainty.

This was an approach that was used in Becker's work. In an interview with Verhoeven, he states:

> The real division between Herb [Blumer] and Everett [Hughes] was that Everett always felt, with some justice I am sorry to say, that Herb discouraged people in their research. Because what you learned from him was that somehow it was always very difficult, perhaps if you took fifteen years you could learn a little bit about something, uhh . . . but you needed this deep understanding. That was not a very practical attitude if you wanted to finish a thesis. He was very critical and, in fact, people who did work with him and I can't remember who, now. But they said that in effect what he would say to you is 'You understand that what you are doing is really no good, don't you?'. If you said yes, then he would approve it. If he thought that you thought it was good then he was more troubled. But you see I learned from Everett how to do research in the practical sense. I mean he would read my field notes and the interviews I did and say you should have asked about this. Oh look you see she said so and so. That must mean . . ., and he would make a whole theory out of it. So I learnt practical theorizing not just how to do the interviewing. The practical theory, making ideas out of data I learnt from Everett.
>
> (Verhoeven, 1989, pp. 25–26)

This emphasis on theorizing was not only a key issue for the development of sociological theory, but also in terms of the ways in which symbolic interactionists view society. Some of these issues were explored by Becker, as he commented:

> Well actually, you see I think there probably is a paradigm in sociology and that most of the differences that we make so much of are very trivial, minor differences. Almost everybody for instance agrees on the notion that society consists of people whose actions are orientated towards the expected reactions of others. . . . Society is then people acting together on the basis of those abilities. Period. Acting together has to be understood in the large sense that Blumer explains it in a 1969 article. Involving everything from the level of the two of us to a city, to a country, or a class system. A class system is a way of acting together. In that sense, it's not, for instance, let's say anti-Marxist. I would regard Marxists' presuppositions about the nature of society as things to be investigated. . . . There is obviously lots of work done under the auspices of Marx's theory that I find very congenial, very useful. I'll give you an example, Hobsbawm. You know the British historian, Eric Hobsbawm, his work on primitive working class is quite clearly Marxist in its inspiration and perfectly usable from my point of view.
>
> (Verhoeven, 1989, p. 41)

In this instance, Verhoeven interprets the interconnection of the individual and society as represented in the work of Becker and many of Blumer's other students as a basic characteristic with the individual being central to society. For

Becker, the advantage of working within this tradition was that interactionism did not dictate the areas of study or the concepts to be used. Instead, interactionism sensitized Becker and his associates to examine topics and themes which were of importance to the people who were studied. In that sense, symbolic interactionism influenced the issues and questions that were raised in Becker's work. For example, in the classic study *Boys in White*, Becker and his colleagues (1961) indicate that symbolic interactionist theory lacks a series of concepts that directed their attention to a particular set of phenomena. As a consequence, the approach that was taken when conducting empirical studies was described in the following terms:

> We did not have a well-worked-out rationale for these choices. Rather, we went into the field and found ourselves concentrating on certain kinds of phenomena . . . The areas we found ourselves concentrating on were consistent with our general theoretical assumptions but did not flow logically and inevitably from them. We studied those matters which seemed to be of importance to the people we studied.
>
> (Becker *et al.*, 1961, p. 20)

Accordingly, the topics selected for analysis were of interest or concern to the participants in the study and were followed up and linked to other phenomena. In this respect, the theoretical perspective *informed but did not determine* the subject of study.

Similarly, in *Making the Grade*, the use of the concept 'perspective' informs a key question in the study: 'What kinds of perspectives do college students create to deal with their academic work under the conditions of college life?' (Becker *et al.*, 1968, p. 6). Such concepts derived from symbolic interactionism informs Becker's work in studies of medical education and educational organizations and has been taken up in the work of others through studies of professions, professional socialization and the construction and reconstruction of medical reality (Friedson, 1970; Atkinson, 1981).

This approach to sociological study, whereby the theory and method used informs but does not dictate the approach taken by the researcher, was also used by Howard Becker when studying teachers. In an interview with John Cockburn (1984), Becker discussed how he developed his field of interest in his PhD dissertation on school teachers when he stated:

> Well, let's take a specific case – my dissertation. The study of schoolteachers of Chicago. I interviewed sixty schoolteachers. I started out to have a randomly chosen sample and found it was totally impossible to do that. Teachers were very reluctant to talk. I ended up with sixty teachers, some from random samples, some I got to from other ways. I was concerned with three or four major questions, kind of very civil minded straightforward questions that could have come out of any theory of sociology or anthropology. How were the major people they had to deal with in their capacities as teachers? What were the expectations that govern those relationships? What kind of trouble arose, what kinds of

sanctions were applied?; and what their careers were in the sense of movements between various schools that represented different constellations of those relationships. Yeah, I derive some generalizations about the Chicago public school system as a result. How I put them essentially was by seeing, and this is, . . . the thing on which they all agree. Somebody may say, one teacher may say, 'I hate teaching blacks, they are impossible, you can't teach them anything'. Another teacher may say, 'Oh you can teach them, you can't teach them as much as you can middle class white children, but . . .'. Alright, what are you going to agree on, agree with there, is the agreement that these children are more difficult to teach than those children? You can say that in the one case the teacher doesn't know what to do about it and in the second case she does. You build up a picture with all the material.

Howard Becker's work focuses upon teachers' perceptions of the situations in which they are located as well as making detailed observations of their world and their work. This analysis, together with the theoretically informed questions which Becker uses, has influenced the development of his methodology.

Methodological work

The methodological tradition to which Howard Becker has contributed is ethnography, an approach which was based on the use of participant observation and interviews in the anthropological study of small-scale societies. This approach was subsequently developed by sociologists in the study of small-scale urban communities and associated institutions such as factories, hospitals and schools.

Much of Becker's early work was based on interviews with teachers where he did not impose his own sociological framework on the teachers' words and work. Instead, statements were followed up as they arose within these interviews as he states:

> The interviews were oriented around the general question of the problems of being a teacher and were not specifically directed towards discovering feelings about social class differences among students. Since these differences created some of the teachers most pressing problems, they were continually brought up by the interviewees themselves.
>
> (Becker, 1953, p. 452)

In this respect, Becker's work on teachers is directed towards the constraints operating on them in the situations in which they are located.

The interviews that were used took an unstructured form having a research agenda rather than a 'set of questions'. In this way, theory and method come together in the work of Howard Becker as a strategy that is developed to allow teachers to express their views in their own words rather than being directed towards a fixed response within a questionnaire. It is this tradition that has been developed by many educational ethnographers working in Britain and the USA (Spindler, 1982; Woods, 1983).

Similarly, in his work on medical schools, Becker focused on day-to-day events as he explained in an interview with John Cockburn (1984):

> It doesn't mean that you ask specific questions, because I'm not talking about that, or a prosecuting attorney or a police investigator . . . did you do this, this or this, yes or no? But rather focusing on some concrete event and asking people to tell you about it. 'What happened yesterday?' I used to do this when I was studying medical schools. I'd miss a day. 'What happened yesterday?' 'Oh, gee, you should have been here [laughter] such and such happened.' 'Yeah, tell me about it.' You know I can ask questions . . . 'Oh yeah. What did he say? . . . did he really say that? . . .' 'Well, no, he didn't really say that . . .'

Here, Becker examined the way he conducted interviews to obtain substantive data, especially on occasions when he wanted to find out about key issues and events. In these circumstances, the informants were given an opportunity to recall events and provide their perceptions and perspectives on a particular set of circumstances (see Burgess, 1983, especially chapter 4; Burgess, 1993).

Conducting interviews may appear straightforward until a researcher goes into the field. In this setting, different kinds of questions need to be posed in order to elicit data. In such circumstances, the researcher needs a detailed knowledge of a setting to ask questions, while in other settings a naïve approach may be more advantageous. In his conversation with John Cockburn (1984), Becker discussed the ways in which different strategies can be used to conduct interviews:

> Competence in the subject matter you're interviewing about is a double edged . . . you could really get in trouble. Because supposing somebody says to you, 'Well you know such and such', and you don't want to appear stupid, so you say, 'Oh yes', Or in fact you know about it so you say 'Oh yes'. Well you don't know how he was going to tell you about it [laughter]. So it's much better to say, 'Well, pretty little, I'm not too sure, can you tell me about it?' And you'd be surprised how many interviewers are busy projecting an image of competence to the person they're inter-viewing because they don't want to appear stupid. In fact if you appear very competent you can intimidate the person you're interviewing. So I always, I've always played fair with them. Now the real difficulty comes when people know you're not naïve. It wouldn't do for me to go around being naïve about interviewing when I interview people, people just wouldn't believe it. I can say, 'Of course I've done a lot of interviewing but I don't know about the way you do it or you think about it – tell me about it'. And that's obviously true. So I like to appear stupid, not stupid uninformed. I would say, 'Look if I knew the answers to these questions I wouldn't waste my time asking about them'. I joke a lot when interview-ing. You know, I've been joking here, that's the way I talk. I treat an

interview as far as I can really as a conversation. You've done very well that way, because there wasn't any change when you turned the recorder on . . . before and after. Some people, you can listen to them, they'll sit and talk to somebody and then they'll say, 'Well I guess we'd better get the interview started' and then [pseudo-cough] . . . that's completely different, it's a completely different person. That person is being very carefully neutral, asking questions in this kind of disembodied voice – it's very funny.

Within this exchange, Becker highlights the importance of conversation in the practice of interviewing – a strategy that has been discussed by many researchers who study education (Hammersley and Atkinson, 1983; Burgess, 1984a; Powney and Watts, 1987).

A further problem identified by Becker is the subject matter of the interview and the extent to which the interviewer has to deal with familiar situations. This is an issue with which Becker has been concerned when studying the lives of teachers, pupils, undergraduates and medical students in schools and higher education institutions. Such work presents particular difficulties for sociologists who are familiar with the situations they observe. Indeed, Becker demonstrated his awareness of this problem when he remarked:

> We may have understated a little the difficulty of observing contemporary classrooms. It is not just the survey method of educational testing or any of those things that keeps people from seeing what is going on. I think instead that it is first and foremost a matter of it all being so familiar that it becomes impossible to single out events that occur in the classroom as things have occurred. Even when they happen right in front of you . . . it takes a tremendous effort of will and imagination to stop seeing only the things that are conventionally there to be seen.
>
> (Becker, 1971, p. 10)

Here, Becker identifies how the familiarity of schooling and its routines is problematic for the researcher. This theme has also been taken up by George and Louise Spindler. They argue that making the strange familiar is not a task that usually confronts the researcher in educational settings. Rather, it is more important and challenging to make the familiar strange by portraying patterns of interaction, and raising questions about classroom strategies and negotiations. Subsequently, these conceptual themes can be illustrated by empirical evidence which will be familiar to the reader. Indeed, George Spindler commented on this problem in his field notes when he stated:

> I sat in classes for days wondering what there was to 'observe'. Teachers taught, reprimanded, rewarded, while pupils sat at desks, squirming, whispering, reading, writing, staring into space, as they had in my own grade school experience, in my practice teaching in a teacher training programme, and in the two years of public school teaching I had done before World War II.
>
> (Fieldnotes quoted in Spindler and Spindler, 1982, p. 24)

In this sense, Becker, and in turn Spindler, have identified some of the key problems that social scientists working in the field of education face whenever they examine situations in their own culture. This situation has also been explored in greater detail by Delamont (1981) who indicates four ways in which researchers may develop strategies for dealing with the study of familiar situations in schools and classrooms. First, she argues that researchers can focus on the study of unusual, bizarre or different classrooms. Secondly, they can study schools and classrooms in comparative settings. Thirdly, they can examine non-educational settings to give a novel perspective on schools and classrooms. Finally, Delamont suggests researchers can question those aspects of schooling that are taken for granted. Some of these strategies for working in schools and classrooms can be traced back to studies conducted by Howard Becker himself who questioned the ways in which teachers work in schools (Becker, 1952a, 1952b, 1953) and the ways students learn in different educational contexts in higher education institutions (Becker *et al.*, 1961, 1968). Within these studies the theoretical commitment of Becker and his colleagues to the study of educational situations on a day-to-day basis has led to the use of participant observation as the main method of enquiry. Indeed, over the years Becker has contributed broadly to ethnographic work through the development of participant observation and in-depth interviews. The way in which this approach is used by Becker is well summarized in his outline of the conduct of participant observation:

> The participant observer gathers data by participating in the daily life of the people or organization he studies. He watches the people he is studying to see in what situations they ordinarily meet and how they behave in them. He enters into conversation with some or all of the participants in these situations and discovers their interpretations of the events he has observed.
>
> (Becker, 1958, p. 652)

Here, Becker points to some key attributes of doing ethnographic research and conducting participant observation. First, he points to the way in which participant observation involves researchers observing the daily life of those who are being studied. In this respect, rich detailed data are collected on the basis of observations in natural settings. Secondly, he points to the importance of obtaining accounts of social situations in the words of the participants that are being observed. Finally, Becker indicates that ethnographic enquiry and participant observation involves much more than merely doing observational work, but also includes the use of conversation, and in turn informal interviews. In this respect, Becker is involved in discussing how the ethnographer's craft can be developed, and ways in which observation and interviews can be utilized in the context of studying schools and schooling. However, Becker's interest in the development of ethnographic enquiry has not been confined to participant observation and interviewing. Other aspects of social research methodology, such as the life history method, have been explored through his commentary (Becker, 1966) on Clifford Shaw's classic study *The Jack Roller* (Shaw, 1930), while his recent analysis of the case study explores another method of investigation that is commonly used in sociological research in general (Becker, 1992) and the study of education in particular (Burgess and Rudduck, 1993).

However, it is an over-simplification to restrict Becker's contribution on methodology to aspects of data collection. As Becker rightly states, it is important to consider data collection in relation to data analysis, and in turn to ways data analysis influences, and is influenced by, the process of writing (Becker, 1986). In this respect, one of his major contributions to research methodology is a discussion of the analysis of qualitative data in the study of Kansas medical school (Becker and Geer, 1960). Here, Becker and Geer examine the way in which sequential analysis is conducted during field research and the strategy and style for reporting conclusions. Most importantly, they indicate that there are no rules for analysing qualitative data (Bryman and Burgess, 1994). Nevertheless, they do point to the importance of maintaining careful records of field data. This is highlighted in a number of studies that Becker has conducted where detailed extracts from field notes are provided. In the classic study *Boys in White* (Becker *et al.*, 1961), numerous fieldwork extracts are provided throughout the text to illustrate conceptual themes. However, Becker and his colleagues are quick to remind the reader at the beginning of the study that these extracts are derived from over 5000 pages of field notes. As a consequence, they remind us of the problems associated with data analysis when they state:

> A technical problem arises in considering how one can be sure that all the items of evidence have been considered; it would clearly be impractical to search through 5000 pages of notes every time one wished to check a proposition. To avoid this, we indexed our field notes and labelled each entry with code numbers referring to major topics under which the given item might be considered. These entries were then reassembled by code number so that we had in one place all the facts bearing on a given topic, thus making possible a relatively quick check of our data on any given point.
>
> (Becker *et al.*, 1961, p. 32)

This approach to qualitative data analysis has been used by Becker to provide insights from fieldwork. These days, researchers are still confronted with similar problems, but many use software programs that have been developed for the analysis of qualitative data and perform similar strategies for handling these data (Fielding and Lee, 1991). Nevertheless, Howard Becker has produced a series of empirical studies that provide important conceptual insights on a range of educational settings.

Sociological insights on education

Unlike many other contributions to the sociology of education, Howard Becker's work encompasses a broad view of education and educational processes and it is not simply confined to schools and schooling (Burgess, 1984b, 1986). Instead, Becker provides insights into a range of educational events and circumstances effecting teachers, pupils, schools, and higher education institutions. These studies have been used by a range of sociologists for their conceptual leads as well as their substantive findings on teachers (Acker, 1989), on medical students and medical education (Atkinson, 1981), on higher education institutions and the development of academic disciplines (Becher, 1989). In addition, Becker's work has also been of interest for the insights that he derives from symbolic interactionism and applies to a range of different educational settings. There are many concepts that sociologists have developed from Becker's work. Among some of the most significant are the use of 'perspectives', 'situational adjustment' and 'the ideal pupil' to which we now turn.

Perspectives

Within the study *Boys in White* (Becker *et al.*, 1961) the concept 'perspective' is used to analyse the collective actions of groups. A perspective is defined as:

> . . . a co-ordinated set of ideas and actions a person uses in dealing with some problematic situation . . . a person's ordinary way of thinking and feeling about and acting in such a situation. These thoughts and actions are co-ordinated in the sense that the actions flow reasonably, from the actor's perspective, from the ideas contained in the perspective. Similarly, the ideas can be seen by an observer to be one of the possible sets of ideas which might form the underlying rationale for the person's actions and are seen by the actor as providing a justification for acting as he does.
>
> (Becker *et al.*, 1961, p. 34)

Perspectives, therefore, come into existence when group members share a common goal in a situation. In this respect, this concept has been used by Becker to explore the way in which groups work out perspectives. In particular, Becker and his colleagues drew attention to the importance of the 'clinical experience perspective' in organizing the views of staff and students which they summarized in the following terms (Becker *et al.*, 1961, p. 242):

1 It is important for a doctor to have had clinical experience.
2 School activities are good in so far as they give students the opportunity to acquire clinical experience or give them access to the clinical experience of their teachers; they are bad when they furnish neither of these things.
3 A student is making real progress toward his goal of preparing for practice when he can demonstrate to himself and others that he has absorbed some lessons from clinical experience; conversely, he has cause to be worried over his own abilities when he fails to absorb such lessons.

They found in their study that they had data which demonstrated how students held this perspective and organized their lives in accordance with it. This idea has been deployed by many sociologists in studying teacher and pupil strategies and perspectives in schools and classrooms (Woods, 1979, 1980; Delamont, 1983). This work has also been developed in specialist subject areas such as physical education. For example, Sparkes (1988) has used the term 'perspective' to examine ways in which an 'academic' perspective is translated into a 'sporting' perspective in the context of physical education. In turn, Sparkes also explores the way in which an 'idealist' perspective was deployed through the promotion of personal and social development in educational gymnastics and swimming. In this way, Sparkes uses Becker's notion of perspective to explore competing views in a physical education department just as others have examined competing views in schools (Hargreaves, 1986).

Situational adjustment

Howard Becker has provided an approach to change when discussing situational adjustment. He summarizes this approach when he states:

> Situations occur in institutions: stable institutions provide stable situations in which little change takes place. When the institutions themselves change, the situations they provide for their participants shift and necessitate development of new patterns of belief and action. When, for instance, a university decides to upgrade its academic programme and begins to require more and different kinds of work from students they must adjust to the new contingencies with which the change confronts them.
>
> (Becker, 1964, p. 45)

It is adjustment of this sort which is seen as one part of the process of adult socialization. In studying teacher socialization, Lacey (1977) includes 'situational adjustment' under the broad heading of social strategy where two varieties of situational adjustment are involved. First, strategic compliance whereby the individual complies with an authority figure's definition of the situation and the constraints involved. Secondly, internalized adjustment where the individual complies with the constraints and believes they are for the best. Indeed, in Lacey's study of the socialization of teachers, he indicates the extent to which he has relied on the work of Becker and the extent to which he has deployed Becker's concepts in his work as shown in Table 1. Here, Lacey demonstrates how concepts that are embedded in the work of Becker and his colleagues have been utilized, modified and deployed within his study of student teacher socialization (Lacey, 1977) by defining and redefining them during fieldwork and data analysis. However, Becker's concepts can also be further explored and developed as Hargreaves demonstrates when he extends the concept of situational adjustment into situational vulnerability (Hargreaves, 1986).

Table 1   The use of Becker's conceptual work in Colin Lacey's socialization of teachers

Becker et al.	Redefinition for this study
Culture	Definition accepted.
Sub-culture	Difference with culture made explicit – used to illuminate the sub-cultural differentiation of student culture on subject discipline lines.
Latent culture	Definition accepted.
Perspective	Accepted but modified to exclude action.
Situational perspective	Accepted but once again the 'action' outcomes are excluded.
Social strategy – not used	New concept developed to include 'action' and 'purpose' of actor.
Situational adjustment	Accepted but subsumed under social strategy as a type of strategy – also sub-divided into strategic compliance and internalized adjustment.
Strategic redefinition – not used	New concept. Another sub-type of social strategy in which the actor is active in changing the socializing institution.

Source: Lacey, 1977, p. 74.

The ideal pupil

On the basis of interviews and discussions with teachers, Becker found that teachers developed the concept of the ideal pupil who was interested in lessons and worked hard, was well dressed and behaved well in classes. He argues, teachers could deal effectively with these pupils. This notion of the 'ideal pupil' has been developed and explored in several studies including Pollard's analysis of primary school pupils (Pollard, 1985). Here, Pollard begins with Becker's analysis of social class variation and the teacher–pupil relationship which involves an ideal matching model. This model was summarized by Becker in the following terms:

> The major problems of workers in the service occupations are likely to be a function of their relationship to their clients or customers, those for whom or on whom the occupational service is performed. Members of such occupations typically have some image of the 'ideal' client and these use this fiction to fashion their conceptions of how their work ought to be performed, and their actual work techniques. To the degree that actual clients approximate this ideal, the worker has no 'client problem'. In a highly differentiated urban society, however, clients vary greatly, and ordinarily only some fraction of the total of potential clients will be 'good' ones. Workers tend to classify clients by the way they vary from this ideal.
> (Becker, 1952a, p. 451)

Within his own study, Pollard uses the notion of the ideal pupil to suggest that, for teacher, the ideal is the child who is supportive of teachers' interests and enables them to cope. As a consequence, he suggests that if Becker is right about the ideal pupil role, then other children are classified and typed by the ways in which they vary from this ideal – a topic that has been explored in further studies. The work of Howard Becker has been used as a conceptual starting point for sociologists of education to explore a variety of social processes associated with educational issues and questions. Indeed, it is common to find concepts developed by Howard Becker being explored in the work of experienced researchers (Woods, 1990) as well as in studies conducted by postgraduates who are writing in the ethnographic tradition.

Conclusion

Howard Becker's work on education is located in the theoretical tradition of symbolic interactionism and the methodological perspective surrounding ethnography. The key advantage to Becker's work is that it can be utilized in a variety of educational circumstances. The methodological approach has been developed in a range of educational contexts so that data collection and data analysis become a creative process in the study of educational settings. However, it is Becker's substantive interests in teachers, students, schools and higher education institutions that continue to be crucial in the development of the sociology of education. Many of these topics can continue to be investigated using Becker's findings as a benchmark against which subsequent empirical studies may be compared. Howard Becker's work is as relevant for sociology and sociologists in the 1990s as it was when it was first published in the 1950s and 1960s. For example, his analyses of teachers' work can be extended and used to examine educational settings as places of work. Secondly, his ideas on labelling, grading and assessment can be used to systematically study examining, not only in schools, but also in higher education institutions. Thirdly, his ideas on deviance (Becker, 1963) can be applied to studies of disruption, disorder, pupil labelling, and social control in schools. In this respect, the work of Howard Becker does not merely relate to educational circumstances at a particular point in time in the USA. Instead, the conceptual and methodological developments associated with his work can be applied to a range of educational settings in a variety of locations. The power of his work is that it can be used to develop our understanding of social situations and social processes when studying teachers, pupils, schools and higher education institutions.

PART 1

Schools, Teachers and Pupils

1 Schools and Systems of Social Status*

Editor's commentary

A central feature of sociological studies of educational systems has been the relationship between education, social stratification and social mobility. In this chapter, Howard Becker examines the relationship between schools and systems of social stratification by comparing the experience of American schools with those in other societies.

Among the key questions to be addressed are: How do schools affect social mobility? How does school organization act on stratification systems? In addition, Becker also begins to look at teachers' careers by asking: What kinds of teachers do schools of various types tend to get?

Within this chapter, Becker argues that schools operate in terms of the status and social class of the societies in which they exist with the result that education can be used as a means of mobility for the disadvantaged and as a means of status maintenance for dominant groups. He concludes that further work is required on the social forces orientating educational institutions.

In most complex societies, and particularly those organized in terms of the values and institutions of Western culture, schools tend to play an important role in the drama of social mobility. Education being at the same time a symbol of social position and a means by which higher position may be achieved, the amount of access to it is one of the keys to the amount of mobility possible in a society. Research on the American school system has alerted us to some of the ways in which schools tend to aid or hinder mobility on the part of subordinate groups.[1] In this paper, I compare the American situation with what is known

* Paper read at the seminar on Group Conflict held at the Institute of Social and Economic Research, University College of the West Indies, Jamaica, August 9–13, 1954. I would like to acknowledge the substantial debt this essay owes to the thinking of Everett G. Hughes and thank David Reisman for his critical reading of an earlier version. Originally published in *Phylon* (1955), pp. 159–70.

of the educational systems of colonial and underdeveloped areas, with an eye to tracing some of the more general dimensions of this relationship between schools and systems of social stratification.

It must be said immediately that in many areas of the world this whole question of mobility and education may be irrelevant. In the first place, education is not often sufficient in itself to make mobility possible. Other things are needed, and a person who acquires a schooling has only begun to move. How far he gets depends, among other things, on where there is to go. If there are no available positions in the upper strata, as there are not in many colonial societies, no way of earning a living in a properly prestigeful way, schooling does not produce mobility but only frustrates desire; it has no effect on the status system. In such a situation disappointment may be avoided by ignoring the mobility possibility.

This raises another qualification limiting the applicability of our analysis. The degree to which mobility is desired by members of subordinate groups cannot be taken for granted but must rather be regarded as problematic. To the degree that such groups consider mobility in fact impossible it will not be sought. Equally important, to the degree that a subordinate group maintains a self-sufficient culture and shares only a minimum of common understanding with those above it – to the degree that the society is what Dr M.G. Smith has termed a 'plural society'[2] – mobility will be sought only within the group: movement to the culturally alien superordinate group will be neither desired nor pursued. Under these circumstances the school has little effect on systems of status, since mobility between groups, however accomplished, is not an important feature of the society.

Within the limits suggested by these qualifications, i.e., in so far as mobility is considered worth attempting and is aided by exposure to schooling, it becomes pertinent to inquire into the ways in which schools affect mobility. In succeeding sections I consider a number of ways in which school organizations, through their institutional structure, act on the stratification system. (Systems in which openly discriminatory law and practice prevent subordinate groups from gaining access to schooling have not been dealt with, their workings being too obvious to require discussion, although perhaps of major importance in any assessment of the current situation.)

I

Societies vary in degree and kind of cultural heterogeneity, and in the way in which these various cultures are taken account of by the school system. In the United States there is, of course, tremendous cultural diversity: ethnic mixture, rural–urban differences, and, in the larger cities, particularly, well developed social–class subcultures, with characteristic emphases in language, thought, behavior, and values.[3]

Underdeveloped areas, while they do not often exhibit the ethnic variety of the metropolitan centers, tend toward a much more radical gap between the cultures of dominant and subordinate groups. Class cultures in European and American cities, greatly though they differ, are grown from the same root. Ethnic differences, while they may be considerable, tend for the most part to be variants of Western European culture. In colonies, established when Europeans migrated and set up governments incorporating the earlier inhabitants of the territory and perhaps other people brought from still elsewhere, the groups may come from two totally different civilizations, as when Europeans met Asians; or Europeans may come into contact with people still living a tribal life, as in Africa. The groups are fewer, the cultures more distinctive, and the distance between much greater.

Not all of these cultures are taken account of and made the basis of practice in the educational institutions that arise in either of these situations. And so the question arises, as Tax puts it,[4] 'whose cultural tradition is to be transmitted?' In the cities of America and Europe there is ordinarily some basic ethnic tradition which, without argument, becomes the medium and content of educational activity. (There may occasionally be two, as in the case of the French and English in Quebec; or the Flemings and Walloons in Belgium.) Education in this culture is available and those wishing something else for their children must make their own provisions. Of the social-class cultures, that of the middle class (in which most educational personnel have their origin[5]) is usually made the standard.

In the colonies and underdeveloped areas, this issue is not so simple. Those at the top waver between wanting everyone else to learn their language and culture, and either of the two opposites of providing no education at all or education more or less within the framework of the native culture. It is easier to rule and to run economic enterprises where native cultures are abandoned for that of the ruling power, for the difficulties in operating Western legal systems and industrial organizations in the midst of an alien culture are tremendous.[6] This implies schools teaching the rulers' culture, in their tongue. On the other hand, the dominant group may take seriously the anthropologists' warnings about the consequences of disrupting the subordinate group's culture in this way. They may feel a sympathy for, or be fascinated by, a primitive and exotic way of life. If it is felt that the values of maintaining the native culture ought to be combined with progress of some sort, vernacular schools may be set up; or, if no such combination is sought, the solution might be no schools at all for the subordinate group. This latter possibility is, in effect, what occurs in those places in which a small elite endeavors to retain its position through a monopoly of education, as in Haiti.

The subordinate group may take one of several attitudes toward this question, to the degree that it interests them at all. They may desire strongly education in the culture of the dominant group because of the status advantages with which they know it can equip them. As in Ireland, and more recently in Africa, they may be caught up in a developing nationalism and wish to reject the dominant culture, uniting the institution of the school with their own language and culture. Where the subject people have their own civilization with well-developed schools holding a ritually-sanctioned status in the society, as in India, resistance to Western education may be led by the teachers of these schools, whose jobs and social position would be lost in the change.[7] Because some knowledge of the culture and more especially the language of the ruling power has been essential if one was to better himself, the dominant attitude has usually been a desire for as much education in that area as could be obtained.

The educator faces a real dilemma in such situations, where subordinate groups require training in the dominant culture for social 'success'. If, on the one hand, teaching proceeds within the cultural and linguistic framework of the dominant group, members of the subordinate group, who have not had the preparation in daily experience presupposed by such an educational program, do not do well. It bears no relation to their daily life, is unfamiliar, difficult to understand, largely meaningless, and can be learned only by rote if at all. This seems to be one of the major problems in Africa,[8] where the African must attempt to acquire a British education, as it is in the cities of the United States, where the lower-class child must try to absorb the teaching of a school oriented to the quite different culture of the middle-class.[9] The problem of motivation is likewise important. As Davis points out, the urban American lower-class child is likely to believe that education will not do him much good, that it is not really worth trying and will not make the effort needed to surmount the obstacles of an unfamiliar culture.[10] (This, of course, is no problem in colonial areas, except to the extent that compulsory education becomes a reality and students are recruited who must be kept in school against their will.) In such situations the child of the subordinate group gets little education: the school may stick determinedly to the alien agenda, but it does not accomplish much. The students learn little that will help them better their social position.

On the other hand, if an attempt is made to adapt the curriculum to the language and/or culture of the subordinate group, in the hope of increasing the achievement of the school, they are likely to interpret the move as an attempt to prevent them from learning what they need to know and acquiring the diplomas they need to get ahead in the world. If, for example, a colonial school is taught in dialect rather than standard English, it may do more teaching; but the students and their families may feel, possibly with some justification, that this only prevents them from learning the language of the dominant group, precisely what they require for successful mobility. Attempts to introduce 'native' subjects and dialects, to provide education different in any way from what would be given a child of the dominant group, are interpreted as an attempt to make sure that the man on the bottom stays there, and may in fact have this consequence, intended or not.[11] For such systems of dual education may easily turn into segregated deadends for the racial or otherwise subordinate groups they are intended to aid. It is for this reason that labor unions in the United States have traditionally opposed plans to build technical secondary schools for working class areas, interpreting this as a move to deny the sons of workers the education they need to rise out of the working class. This even where the ordinary secondary school proceeds in a manner that makes it difficult for the lower-class child to succeed.

In addition, teachers in such areas are likely themselves to be mobile from the subordinate group, one sign of their successful mobility being their ease in the language and cultural ways of the dominant group. They are likely to reject efforts to get them to teach in a language or dialect carrying less prestige.[12]

In short, educators in culturally differentiated societies are caught on the horns of this dilemma: to bring education 'down' to the level of the subordinate group and thus give something, but not very much, to all, or to 'maintain standards' and thus aid only the gifted few? In whichever direction they move, they are likely to end by perpetuating the cultural differences between groups, and slowing the mobility flow to the continuing disadvantage of those at the bottom.

(By focusing only on mobility, this kind of argument ignores the importance of the school's function as the transmitter of a valued cultural heritage. From a different perspective than the rather one-sided one of this paper, one might raise questions about the fate of this important function in school systems faced with these problems.)

II

Not all societies are organized so as easily to accommodate schools fashioned on the Western model. The question of whether a society can support such institutions involves not only the financial problems which are everywhere a concern of educational administrators, but also the questions of the degree to which the society's values mesh with the notion of formal education and the extent to which they can furnish personnel to man the schools.

Although there are many failures of modern Western societies to support fully formal education, these societies do accept the notion of education of all children up to some specified age and pattern social arrangements in such a way as to allow this to go on. In many of the world's underdeveloped areas, on the other hand, particularly those in which subordinate groups are still organized at the tribal level, the very notion of a school is foreign to the accepted way of life. In addition, the child is an economic asset on which the family depends. Schooling, because it ties up a potential worker in non-productive activity, is expensive for them even when it is free. Consequently, attendance is erratic, always at the mercy of family need.

One result of the lack of cultural support of the educational enterprise in either kind of area is that education cannot be really cumulative, cannot progress year by year to new and higher subjects and skills. The teacher can never count on his pupils having already mastered some set of facts or skills just because they have had so-and-so many years of schools, and each year tends to become a repetition of the last, devoted to attempting to make sure that everyone has at least mastered the basic skills of reading and writing. At each higher grade level the gap between what should be learned and what actually is learned becomes greater; teaching degenerates into a desperate attempt to instill some minimum amount of learning. Teachers are tempted in such a discouraging situation to take the easy way out, either giving up completely or devoting their efforts only to those few students who will accept them wholeheartedly and are comparatively easy to teach. The teachers' stereotypes about the subordinate group's lack of ability tend to be confirmed by their experience and leads to less effort being expended where more is in fact required, thus increasing the school's failure.

The question of financial support is of course important. Within the limits imposed by the extent of the society's resources – and these are immensely limiting in an area such as Africa where the money is simply not available to do the job – the problem is one of the allocation of funds. How much are people willing to pay to have children educated, particularly where schools are supported through taxation and the person who pays the largest taxes finds himself subsidizing the education of children of the subordinate group? Hughes has suggested that Canadian public education suffers from the reluctance of the smaller group of well-to-do English to so subsidize the education of the poorer and more numerous French Canadians.[13] The same political problems of the allocation of funds, rooted in the relations of status groups, are found in the segregated schools of the southern United States, and in those cities in which residential segregation makes possible selective spending for the education of racial and social-class minorities. Such financial dilemmas tend to be resolved to the disadvantage of subordinate groups.

Finally, there is the question of providing sufficient adequately trained personnel to keep the institution operating. What incentives are available to induce people of the desired kind to become teachers and are they sufficient to do the job? This may be put in terms of what might be called career potential. Starting as a teacher, where can one go, and are these prospects attractive enough to those who might enter the profession? In the United States, there are many people with appropriate education. From these, it appears that teachers are drawn largely from the ranks of those of limited ambition, who prefer the relative security of the school teacher's restricted occupational horizon to the risks of occupations which allow for more movement up and down. There are a great many people possessing this combination of limited ambition and higher education, and teachers are recruited in sizeable numbers.

In the underdeveloped areas, on the other hand, anyone who perseveres enough to get the education necessary for teaching wants a greater reward for his effort. And such rewards are often available. In Africa and India, better careers in industry and government were available to English speaking school graduates. Few received the basic education necessary for teacher training; they were ambitious, and passed up teaching for these alternative careers which carried more prestige, paid better, and tended to be nearer the centers of population.[14] This meant, in the first place, a shortage of teachers. Second, when coupled with the inevitable desire of educational authorities to get people with the highest educational qualifications, it meant that teachers tended to be those who had failed in a try for the bigger prizes. 'There has been (in India) a tendency to prefer "failed matriculates" ready for the sake of a living to face work and surroundings with which they are out of sympathy, to less advanced, but more appropriate candidates.'[15] A system which thus almost deliberately selects disgruntled failures for its teachers is bound not to get the greatest amount of teaching enthusiasm, which may be more important than a degree.

It may be taken for granted that where teachers are difficult to recruit, those groups that they dislike teaching – the subordinate ones – will get something less than their share. Any system faced with a real shortage of teachers, therefore, will operate in such a way as to reduce the possibility of upward mobility for these groups, and it is only where an institutional system has been devised that will recruit successfully that this tendency is reversed. It is clear that different kinds of incentives and potential careers than those made available by the bureaucratic seniority systems of the older countries must be utilized in the underdeveloped areas if recruitment is to be successful.

III

Individual schools are linked, formally or otherwise, into systems, within whose boundaries teachers move from school to school in search of whatever satisfactions they happen to seek in their work. The teacher's career is made up of a series of such movements between schools in the system, each of these constituting a stage in the career.[16] Looking at such a system at any given moment, we see a distribution of teachers at various stages of their careers among the schools making up the system. Systems tend to breed distinctive career patterns and this distribution of teachers of various kinds is not random. The question can thus be raised: what kinds of teachers do schools of various types tend to get?

The first point to be noted is that all schools in such a system do not look alike to the teacher. They differ in the kind of children they have as pupils, in the salaries they pay, in location, and so on. Some schools are very attractive to the teacher, places at which she would like very much to teach, while others are thought of as places to be avoided if possible. It may be, as in Chicago, that lower-class and Negro children are considered hardest to teach and most difficult to handle, so that schools containing them are avoided.[17] It may be, as in many places in the United States, that the teacher attempts to work her way out of the poorer paying, socially constraining rural hinterland into the nearest big city; Kansas City exemplifies this.[18] In underdeveloped areas, generally, living conditions, salaries, prestige, and ease of teaching. all combine to draw teachers toward the centers of population and away from the 'backwoods' areas. For any of the reasons suggested, it is typically the schools handling children of subordinate groups which are least desired, and teachers' careers tend to be structured in terms of movement away from such schools.

Career movements tend to take this pattern, no matter what the arrangements by which movement occurs. In Chicago, teachers may request transfers to other schools, and will be moved as soon as there is a vacancy for which their request is of longest standing; this is essentially an arrangement by which seniority gets one the desired job. The record of these requests, when mapped, shows a tremendous movement away from the slums toward the middle-class areas. The same pattern may be seen in those informal rural–urban systems, like that of Kansas City, in which movement is accomplished by acquiring experience and bargaining successfully for the more desired jobs. In general, those teachers who have what the system wants – experience, teaching ability, whatever it may be – have most choice of position, and this leads to the pattern described.

Such a pattern of movement means that the less desirable schools, those teachers want to avoid, get something less than an equal share of teaching talent. At the least, it typically means that they do not get the experienced teachers, for experience is almost always a ticket to a better job, whether through the workings of a seniority system or through the greater bargaining power it provides in bidding for jobs. In Chicago, many lower-class Negro schools are staffed almost entirely by teachers fresh from training school, the only ones who cannot choose their assignments; as soon as they build up enough seniority to move, they go, to be replaced by a new batch of beginners. More generally, it is probably true that, whatever the qualities a school system wishes to reward in its teachers, those qualities can be effectively rewarded only by assignment to the more desired schools, so that disadvantaged groups, who require the most skilled and experienced teaching, get the opposite and something less than an equal chance to an education.

There is very little information on problems of this order in underdeveloped areas. It seems likely that this picture holds for the West Indies, and for Africa – the poor, the rural folk, those most backward being taught by teachers who, through lack of experience or ability, cannot get positions in the cities. It would be most revealing to see studies made of the aspirations and careers of teachers in such societies, with special emphasis on the fate of enthusiasm and ability in these systems. Is it true here too that careers move in such a way that students of the dominant groups get the best teaching, and vice versa, with the obvious consequences for the mobility chances of the subordinate group?

Such tendencies get reinforced, after they have been operating for any length of time, in a way that makes them very difficult to change. The teachers who have been fortunate enough to locate in what are commonly considered the 'more desirable' schools come to consider these positions to be their inalienable property. They feel that they have 'served their time' (suggestive phrase!) and are now enjoying a well-earned reward. Others look forward to an equal reward when they too have served their time in the less desirable places; careers are built around this expectation. Any attempt to remove teachers from these schools and put them in places where their skills are more needed is looked on with great disfavor, as though the terms of contract were being broken; it may even be regarded as a species of punishment. (It is said that such transfers were used as disciplinary measures in the Chicago schools at one time, in much the same way that policemen are punished by being assigned a beat in the 'sticks.') There are hints of this tendency in Africa. The group reporting on educational problems in East and Central Africa mentions a similar 'uneasiness in the teaching profession at the arbitrariness with which teachers and especially heads of schools are transferred from one school to another . . . Instances were encountered in which a head of a school was transferred to a backward school as soon as his energy had produced an obvious improvement in his present school.'[19] A transfer is arbitrary only when it violates some established expectation, and it appears that such expectations have already begun to form.

IV

Institutions tend to try to become self-contained systems of power and to protect themselves against interference from the outside. Institutions are the means by which society delegates particular functions to specialized groups, always retaining the right to examine and pass judgment on that group's performance. Institutional functionaries feel that they understand the problems involved better than any layman and dislike any potential or actual interference, wanting to be left free to run things in their own way. Consequently, they erect defensive barriers designed to keep outsiders on the outside and prevent the surrounding society from directly affecting the institution's operation.

Schools share this tendency. Teachers and administrators find most satisfaction in their work, and feel that they do their best work, when there is no interference by the layman. They erect such barriers of secrecy and mutual defense. It is likely that the development of such defenses proceeds in relation to the perceived possibility of effective attack from the outside. The independence of the schools from such interference has an important, though by no means always the same, effect on the way the schools affect social mobility patterns.

Educational institutions differ greatly in the degree to which they are likely to be attacked, and in the success of their defense of their autonomy. The Chicago situation presents a fully developed case. These schools are very likely to be attacked at almost any time by the parents of their pupils, for not doing their job well enough or in the right way, for using improper disciplinary measures, and so on. They have developed, quite informally, an amazingly strong self-protective code. No principal or teacher ought ever to admit that anyone on the school staff has done anything wrong, even if this necessitates open lying, for to admit such a thing would be to admit the parents into the power structure of the school. The fact that anything has gone wrong is a closely kept secret. Parents and other outsiders are allowed to see the schools in action only when there is plenty of warning and a 'show' of some kind has been prepared for them.[20] In systems oriented more toward examination systems of one kind or another, the possibility of attack may produce in addition an emphasis on demonstrable results – a high proportion of passes, for instance – even when this must be achieved by using rote learning methods in preference to more substantial kinds of education.

Such a system does not work equally well with all kinds of people. In Chicago, it works to perfection with lower-class parents who are easily intimidated by middle-class institutions. But it does not work well at all with the middle-class parent, who knows how to make trouble for the school and will do so without compunction if not satisfied.

Along with these two possibilities – that attacks will be successfully defended against, or that defense will fail – is a third: that there is no danger of attack and no need of defense. This may be the case in some of the newer colonies in which the parents are relatively unable to assess the school's work and deal with educational authorities. (It is always possible, however, that groups from outside the society whose opinion carries weight will play the role that parents do elsewhere.) It is likely, in colonial situations, that such attacks as are made will be focused more on quantitative concerns – numbers of schools and teachers, etc. – and that the brunt of any attack will be borne not by the teacher but by those administrative officers in charge of running the whole system.

In any case, whether by protective arrangements or through freedom from attack, the schools may gain for themselves an almost free hand, so that the teachers can pursue their real purpose relatively unhampered. In a system like Chicago's, particularly in lower-class areas, the teacher's primary aim is just to get along and not have too much trouble; educational standards come second. It is only where the institutional defenses are breached, as they are in middle-class areas, that this can be avoided and educational standards maintained. One of the elements preventing the lower-class from receiving the full benefits of education in a class society is its lack of organization and effectiveness in pushing teachers to do better work. Where, on the other hand, public demand is for quantity rather than quality, as may be the case in Africa, a determined teaching group able to withstand attack may actually provide more lasting benefit to underprivileged groups.

Again, such a public may be effective in forcing the schools to give out symbols of achievement whether or not there has been any achievement in fact; this is probably particularly the case in status-conscious underdeveloped societies, where the certificate or degree is almost a passport to higher position; see, for example, Tugwell's description of the University of Puerto Rico where, at one time, students demanded and got, from a vulnerable faculty, degrees without accomplishment.[21] These can be hollow victories for the native group where, as in Africa and India, some real learning – at least, of a new language – must occur, where the symbols of accomplishment without the fact do no good.

The results of the educator's effort to run his enterprise in his own way, with no interference from outside, is thus quite important for the kind of education the child receives and the amount of social mobility made possible. The specific effect in any situation depends on three variables: the desires of parents and others who may possibly wish to have a voice in the school's operation; the desires of teachers and educational administrators; and the way in which the conflict over control of the schools is resolved, either in such a way as to make them more responsive to outside pressure or so as to preserve for them effective autonomy.

V

The schools, then, function importantly in the operation of the system of status and social class of the societies in which they exist. Where a society contains disadvantaged groups, education is one of the possible means of mobility for them just as it is one of the means by which members of the dominant group maintain their status. Education can provide a sizeable amount of opportunity for disadvantaged groups, if all groups have an equal chance to get an education.

It has been the concern of this paper to point out the ways in which the ordinary operation of educational institutions, quite apart from deliberately discriminatory measures, tends to cut down the amount of mobility opportunity the schools provide. Its major thesis is that in solving such problems as the recruitment and distribution of personnel, the defense of institutional autonomy, etc., the schools, organized in terms of one of the sub-cultures of a heterogeneous society, tend to operate in such a way that members of subordinate groups of differing culture do not get their fair share of educational opportunity, and thus of opportunity for social mobility.

If it is true that the schools tend to have this conservative effect in general, it is of great importance, both theoretically and practically, to search for and investigate systematically such situations as that which existed, for example, in various cities of the United States at various times, in which the schools functioned in the opposite direction, becoming great channels of mobility for large groups. More research is needed on cases of this kind in order to bring out more fully the basic forces at work in orienting educational institutions toward one or another of these modes of relation to status system.

Notes

1. On the American situation in general, see Warner, Havighurst and Loeb (1944). I have relied heavily on the studies of the Chicago School system done under the direction of Everett C. Hughes, reported in a number of MA and PhD theses at the University of Chicago, as well as in three papers by the present author (Becker, 1952a, 1952b and 1953).
2. See Smith (1953, 1954).
3. On the differences between lower- and middle-class behaviour and values, Davis (1946) and Schatzman and Strauss (1955).
4. Tax (1946).
5. Cf. Warner, Havighurst and Loeb (1944).
6. Maunier (1949); on industrial systems see Hughes (1952) chapter 5.
7. See Cunningham (1941).
8. Batten (1948), p. 66. See also J.M. van der Kroef's (1954) description of a classical case of the effect of this problem on the school's mobility function in Indonesia, both before and after independence from the Dutch had been achieved.
9. Cf. Davis (1950), Eells *et al.* (1951).
10. Davis (1946).
11. Cf. Mayhew (1926), p. 71.
12. Cf. Leyburn (1941), p. 279.
13. Hughes (1943). Chapter 11. Professor Hughes has made the same point more strongly in lectures at the University of Chicago.
14. Cunningham (1941), pp. 150, 160; Batten (1953), pp. 43–7; Nuffield Foundation and the Colonial Office (1953), p. 37.

15. Mayhew (1926), p. 250.
16. On careers, see Hughes (1937), 404–13 and Hall (1948).
17. Becker (1952a).
18. I draw here on an unpublished study of Kansas City teachers by Warren Peterson.
19. The Nuffield Foundation and the Colonial Office (1953), p. 117.
20. Summarized from Becker (1953) and from material in the PhD thesis of Mac-Dowell (1954).
21. Tugwell (1947), p. 109.

2 Social-Class Variations in the Teacher–Pupil Relationship*

Editor's commentary

This chapter was originally published in the Journal of Educational Sociology *in 1952. The analysis links with work that was being conducted during this period on social class and educational opportunity. However, Howard Becker extends this topic area by focusing on teacher–pupil interaction.*

There have been many studies of teacher–pupil interaction in schools and classrooms over the last 25 years, based on observation and participant observation as well as interviews with teachers and pupils. Many of these studies demonstrate that the authors are indebted to Howard Becker's work on the ways in which teachers observe, classify and react to pupil behaviour.

This chapter is based on a study of 60 teachers in Chicago schools. The chapter draws on interviews with these teachers and quotations are taken from the interview transcripts to examine the problems of teaching, discipline and the moral acceptability of pupils.

The major problems of workers in the service occupations are likely to be a function of their relationship to their clients or customers, those for whom or on whom the occupational service is performed.[1] Members of such occupations typically have some image of the 'ideal' client, and it is in terms of this fiction that they fashion their conceptions of how their work ought to be performed, and their actual work techniques. To the degree that actual clients approximate this ideal the worker will have no 'client problem.'

In a highly differentiated urban society, however, clients will vary greatly, and ordinarily only some fraction of the total of potential clients will be 'good' ones. Workers tend to classify clients in terms of the way in which they vary

* This chapter is based on research done under a grant from the Committee on Education, Training and Research in Race Relations at the University of Chicago. Originally published in the *Journal of Educational Sociology* (1952), 25: 451–65.

from this ideal. The fact of client variation from the occupational ideal emphasizes the intimate relation of the institution in which work is carried on to its environing society. If that society does not prepare people to play their client roles in the manner desired by the occupation's members there will be conflicts, and problems for the workers in the performance of their work. One of the major factors affecting the production of suitable clients is the cultural diversity of various social classes in the society. The cultures of particular social-class groups may operate to produce clients who make the worker's position extremely difficult.

We deal here with this problem as it appears in the experience of the functionaries of a large urban educational institution, the Chicago public school system, discussing the way in which teachers in this system observe, classify and react to class-typed differences in the behavior of the children with whom they work. The material to be presented is thus relevant not only to problems of occupational organization but also to the problem of differences in the educational opportunities available to children of various social-classes. Warner, Havighurst and Loeb[2] and Hollingshead[3] have demonstrated the manner in which the schools tend to favor and select out children of the middle classes. Allison Davis has pointed to those factors in the class cultures involved which make lower-class children less and middle-class children more adaptable to the work and behavioral standards of the school.[4] This paper will contribute to knowledge in this area by analyzing the manner in which the public school teacher reacts to these cultural differences and, in so doing, perpetuates the discrimination of our educational system against the lower-class child.

The analysis is based on sixty interviews with teachers in the Chicago system.[5] The interviews were oriented around the general question of the problems of being a teacher and were not specifically directed toward discovering feelings about social-class differences among students. Since these differences created some of the teachers' most pressing problems they were continually brought up by the interviewees themselves. They typically distinguished three social-class groups with which they, as teachers, came in contact: (1) a bottom stratum, probably equivalent to the lower-lower and parts of the upper-lower class; (2) an upper stratum, probably equivalent to the upper-middle class; and (3) a middle stratum, probably equivalent to the lower-middle and parts of the upper-lower class. We will adopt the convention of referring to these groups as lower, upper and middle groups, but it should be understood that this terminology refers to the teachers' classification of students and not to the ordinary sociological description.

We will proceed by taking up the three problems that loomed largest in the teachers' discussion of adjustment to their students: (1) the problem of *teaching* itself, (2) the problem of *discipline*, and (3) the problem of the *moral acceptability* of the students. In each case the variation in the form of and adjustment to the problem by the characteristics of the children of the various class groups distinguished by teachers is discussed.

I

A basic problem in any occupation is that of performing one's given task successfully, and where this involves working with human beings their qualities are a major variable affecting the ease with which the work can be done. The teacher considers that she has done her job adequately when she has brought about an observable change in the children's skills and knowledge which she can attribute to her own efforts:

> Well, I would say that a teacher is successful when she is putting the material across to the children, when she is getting some response from them. I'll tell you something. Teaching is a very rewarding line of work, because you can see those children grow under your hands. You can see the difference in them after you've had them for five months. You can see where they've started and where they've got to. And it's all yours. It really is rewarding in that way, you can see results and know that it's your work that brought those results about.

She feels that she has a better chance of success in this area when her pupils are interested in attending and working hard in school, and are trained at home in such a way that they are bright and quick at school work. Her problems arise in teaching those groups who do not meet these specifications, for in these cases her teaching techniques, tailored to the 'perfect' student, are inadequate to cope with the reality, and she is left with a feeling of having failed in performing her basic task.

Davis has described the orientations toward education in general, and schoolwork in particular, of the lower and middle classes:

> Thus, our educational system, which next to the family is the most effective agency in teaching good work habits to middle class people, is largely ineffective and unrealistic with underprivileged groups. Education fails to motivate such workers because our schools and our society both lack *real rewards* to offer underprivileged groups. Neither lower class children or adults will work hard in school or on the job just to please the teacher or boss. They are not going to learn to be ambitious, to be conscientious, and to study hard, as if school and work were a fine character-building game, which one plays just for the sake of playing. They can see, indeed, that those who work hard at school usually have families that already have the occupations, homes, and social acceptance that the school holds up as the rewards of education. The underprivileged workers can see also that the chances of their getting enough education to make their attainment of these rewards in the future at all probable is very slight. Since they can win the rewards of prestige and social acceptance in their own slum groups without much education, they do not take very seriously the motivation taught by the school.[6]

As these cultural differences produce variations from the image of the 'ideal' student, teachers tend to use class terms in describing the children with whom they work.

Children of the lowest group, from slum areas, are characterized as the most difficult group to teach successfully, lacking in interest in school, learning ability, and outside training:

> They don't have the right kind of study habits. They can't seem to apply themselves as well. Of course, it's not their fault; they aren't brought up right. After all, the parents in a neighborhood like that really aren't interested . . . But, as I say, those children don't learn very quickly. A great many of them don't seem to be really interested in getting an education. I don't think they are. It's hard to get anything done with children like that. They simply don't respond.

In definite contrast are the terms used to describe children of the upper group:

> In a neighborhood like this there's something about the children, you just feel like you're accomplishing so much more. You throw an idea out and you can see that it takes hold. The children know what you're talking about and they think about it. Then they come in with projects and pictures and additional information, and it just makes you feel good to see it. They go places and see things, and they know what you're talking about. For instance, you might be teaching social studies or geography . . . You bring something up and a child says, 'Oh my parents took me to see that in the museum.' You can just do more with material like that.

Ambivalent feelings are aroused by children of the middle group. While motivated to work hard in school they lack the proper out-of-school training:

> Well, they're very nice here, very nice. They're not hard to handle. You see, they're taught respect in the home and they're respectful to the teacher. They want to work and do well . . . Of course, they're not too brilliant. You know what I mean. But they are very nice children and very easy to work with.

In short, the differences between groups make it possible for the teacher to feel successful at her job only with the top group; with the other groups she feels, in greater or lesser measure, that she has failed.

These differences in ability to do school work, as perceived by teachers, have important consequences. They lead, in the first place, to differences in actual teaching techniques. A young high school teacher contrasted the techniques used in 'slum' schools with those used in 'better' schools:

> At S——, there were a lot of guys who were just waiting till they were sixteen so they could get out of school. L——, everybody – well, a very large percentage, I'll say – was going on to secondary school, to college. That certainly made a difference in their classroom work. You had to teach differently at the different schools. For instance, at S——, if you had demonstrations in chemistry they had to be pretty flashy, lots of noise and smoke, before they'd get interested in it. That wasn't necessary at L——. Or at S—— if you were having electricity or something like that you had

to get the static electricity machine out and have them all stand around and hold hands so that they'd all get a little jolt.

Further, the teacher feels that where these differences are recognized by her superiors there will be a corresponding variation in the amount of work she is expected to accomplish. She expects that the amount of work and effort required of her will vary inversely with the social status of her pupils. This teacher compared schools from the extremes of the class range:

> So you have to be on your toes and keep up to where you're supposed to be in the course of study. Now, in a school like the D—— [slum school] you're just not expected to complete all that work. It's almost impossible. For instance, in the second grade we're supposed to cover nine spelling words a week. Well, I can do that up here at the K—— ['better' school], they can take nine new words a week. But the best class I ever had at the D—— was only able to achieve six words a week and they had to work pretty hard to get that. So I never finished the year's work in spelling. I couldn't. And I really wasn't expected to.

One resultant of this situation – in which less is expected of those teachers whose students are more difficult to teach – is that the problem becomes more aggravated in each grade, as the gap between what the children should know and what they actually do know becomes wider and wider. A principal of such a school describes the degeneration there of the teaching problem into a struggle to get a few basic skills across, in a situation where this cumulative effect makes following the normal program of study impossible:

> The children come into our upper grades with very poor reading ability. That means that all the way through our school everybody is concentrating on reading. It's not like at a school like S—— [middle group] where they have science and history and so on. At a school like that they figure that from first to fourth you learn to read and from fifth to eighth you read to learn. You use your reading to learn other material. Well, these children don't reach that second stage while they're with us. We have to plug along getting them to learn to read. Our teachers are pretty well satisfied if the children can read and do simple number work when they leave here. You'll find that they don't think very much of subjects like science, and so on. They haven't got any time for that. They're just trying to get these basic things over . . . That's why our school is different from one like the S——.

Such consequences of teachers' differential reaction to various class groups obviously operate to further perpetuate those class-cultural characteristics to which they object in the first place.

II

Discipline is the second of the teacher's major problems with her students. Willard Waller pointed to its basis when he wrote that 'Teacher and pupil confront each other in the school with an original conflict of desires, and however much that conflict may be reduced in amount, or however much it may be hidden, it still remains.'[7] We must recognize that conflict, either actual or potential, is ever present in the teacher–pupil relationship, the teacher attempting to maintain her control against the children's efforts to break it.[8] This conflict is felt even with those children who present least difficulty; a teacher who considered her pupils models of good behavior nevertheless said:

> But there's that tension all the time. Between you and the students. It's hard on your nerves. Teaching is fun, if you enjoy your subject, but it's the discipline that keeps your nerves on edge, you know what I mean? There's always that tension. Sometimes people say, 'Oh, you teach school. That's an easy job, just sitting around all day long.' They don't know what it's really like. It's hard on your nerves.

The teacher is tense because she fears that she will lose control, which she tends to define in terms of some line beyond which she will not allow the children to go. Wherever she may draw this line (and there is considerable variation), the teacher feels that she has a 'discipline' problem when the children attempt to push beyond it. The form and intensity of this problem are felt to vary from one social-class group to another, as might be expected from Davis' description of class emphases on aggression:

> In general, middle-class aggression is taught to adolescents in the form of social and economic skills which will enable them to compete effectively at that level . . . In lower-class families, physical aggression is as much a normal, socially approved and socially inculcated type of behavior as it is in frontier communities.[9]

These differences in child training are matched by variation in the teachers' reactions.

Children in 'slum' schools are considered most difficult to control, being given to unrestrained behavior and physical violence. The interviews are filled with descriptions of such difficulties. Miriam Wagenschein, in a parallel study of the beginning school teacher, gave this summary of the experiences of these younger teachers in lower-class schools:

> The reports which these teachers give of what *can* be done by a group of children are nothing short of amazing. A young white teacher walked into her new classroom and was greeted with the comment, 'Another damn white one.' Another was 'rushed' at her desk by the entire class when she tried to be extremely strict with them. Teachers report having been bitten, tripped, and pushed on the stairs. Another gave an account of a second grader throwing a milk bottle at the teacher and of a first grader having such a temper tantrum that it took the principal and two policemen to get him out of the room. In another school following a fight on the playground, the principal took thirty-two razor blades from children in a first grade room. Some teachers indicated fear that they might be

attacked by irate persons in the neighborhoods in which they teach. Other teachers report that their pupils carry long pieces of glass and have been known to threaten other pupils with them, while others jab each other with hypodermic needles. One boy got angry with his teacher and knocked in the fender of her car.[10]

In these schools a major part of the teacher's time must be devoted to discipline; as one said: 'It's just a question of keeping them in line.' This emphasis on discipline detracts from the school's primary function of teaching, thus discriminating, in terms of available educational opportunity, against the children of these schools.

Children of the middle group are thought of as docile, and with them the teacher has least difficulty with discipline:

> Those children were much quieter, easier to work with. When we'd play our little games there was never any commotion. That was a very nice school to work in. Everything was quite nice about it. The children were easy to work with . . .

Children of the upper group are felt hard to handle in some respects, and are often termed 'spoiled,' 'overindulged,' or 'neurotic'; they do not play the role of the child in the submissive manner teachers consider appropriate. One interviewee, speaking of this group, said:

> I think most teachers prefer not to teach in that type of school. The children are more pampered and, as we say, more inclined to run the school for themselves. The parents are very much at fault. The children are not used to taking orders at home and naturally they won't take them at school either.

Teachers develop methods of dealing with these discipline problems, and these tend to vary between social-class groups as do the problems themselves. The basic device used by successful disciplinarians is to establish authority clearly on the first meeting with the class:

> You can't ever let them get the upper hand on you or you're through. So I start out tough. The first day I get a new class in, I let them know who's boss . . . You've got to start off tough, then you can ease up as you go along. If you start out easy-going, when you try to get tough they'll just look at you and laugh.

Having once established such a relation, it is considered important that the teacher be consistent in her behavior so that the children will continue to respect and obey her:

> I let them know I mean business. That's one thing you must do. Say nothing that you won't follow through on. Some teachers will say anything to keep kids quiet, they'll threaten anything. Then they can't or won't carry out their threats. Naturally, the children won't pay any attention to them after that. You must never say anything that you won't back up.

In the difficult 'slum' schools, teachers feel the necessity of using stern measures, up to and including physical violence (nominally outlawed):

> Technically you're not supposed to lay a hand on a kid. Well, they don't, technically. But there are a lot of ways of handling a kid so that it doesn't show – and then it's the teacher's word against the kid's, so the kid hasn't got a chance. Like dear Mrs.———. She gets mad at a kid, she takes him out in the hall. She gets him stood up against the wall. Then she's got a way of chucking the kid under the chin, only hard, so that it knocks his head back against the wall. It doesn't leave a mark on him. But when he comes back in that room he can hardly see straight, he's so knocked out. It's really rough. There's a lot of little tricks like that that you learn about.

Where such devices are not used, there is recourse to violent punishment, 'tongue lashings.' All teachers, however, are not emotionally equipped for such behavior and must find other means:

> The worst thing I can do is lose my temper and start raving . . . You've got to believe in that kind of thing in order for it to work . . . If you don't honestly believe it it shows up and the children know you don't mean it and it doesn't do any good anyway . . . I try a different approach myself. Whenever they get too rowdy I go to the piano and . . . play something and we have rhythms or something until they sort of settle down . . . That's what we call 'softsoaping ' them. It seems to work for me. It's about the only thing I can do.

Some teachers may also resort to calling in the parents, a device whose usefulness is limited by the fact that such summonses are most frequently ignored. The teacher's disciplinary power in such a school is also limited by her fear of retaliation by the students: 'Those fellows are pretty big, and I just think it would take a bigger person than me to handle them. I certainly wouldn't like to try.'

In the school with children of the middle group no strong sanctions are required, mild reprimands sufficing:

> Now the children at Z—— here are quite nice to teach. They're pliable, yes, that's the word, they're pliable. They will go along with you on things and not fight you. You can take them any place and say to them, 'I'm counting on you not to disgrace your school. Let's see that Z—— spirit.' And they'll behave for you . . . They can be frightened, they have fear in them. They're pliable, flexible, you can do things with them. They're afraid of their parents and what they'll do to them if they get into trouble at school. And they're afraid of the administration. They're afraid of being sent down to the principal. So that they can be handled.

Children of the upper group often act in a way which may be interpreted as 'misbehavior' but which does not represent a conscious attack on the teacher's authority. Many teachers are able to disregard such activity by interpreting it as a natural concomitant of the 'brightness' and 'intelligence' of such children.

Where such an interpretation is not possible the teachers feel hampered by a lack of effective sanctions:

> I try different things like keeping them out of a gym period or a recess period. But that doesn't always work. I have this one little boy who just didn't care when I used those punishments. He said he didn't like gym anyway. I don't know what I'm going to do with him.

The teacher's power in such schools is further limited by the fact that the children are able to mobilize their influential parents so as to exert a large degree of control over the actions of school personnel.

It should be noted, finally, that discipline problems tend to become less important as the length of the teacher's stay in a particular school makes it possible for her to build a reputation which coerces the children into behaving without attempting any test of strength:[11]

> I have no trouble with the children. Once you establish a reputation and they know what to expect, they respect you and you have no trouble. Of course, that's different for a new teacher, but when you're established that's no problem at all.

III

The third area of problems has been termed that of *moral acceptability*, and arises from the fact that some actions of one's potential clients may be offensive in terms of some deeply felt set of moral standards; these clients are thus morally unacceptable. Teachers find that some of their pupils act in such a way as to make themselves unacceptable in terms of the moral values centered around health and cleanliness, sex and aggression, ambition and work, and the relations of age groups.

Children of the middle group present no problem at this level, being universally described as clean, well dressed, moderate in their behavior, and hard working. Children from the 'better' neighborhoods are considered deficient in the important moral traits of politeness and respect for elders:

> Where the children come from wealthy homes. That's not so good either. They're not used to doing work at home. They have maids and servants of all kinds and they're used to having things done for them, instead of doing them themselves . . . They won't do anything. For instance, if they drop a piece of cloth on the floor, they'll just let it lay, they wouldn't think of bending over to pick it up. That's janitor's work to them. As a matter of fact, one of them said to me once: 'If I pick that up there wouldn't be any work for the janitor to do.' Well, it's pretty difficult to deal with children like that.

Further, they are regarded as likely to transgress what the teachers define as moral boundaries in the matter of smoking and drinking; it is particularly shocking that such 'nice' children should have such vices.

It is, however, the 'slum' child who most deeply offends the teacher's moral sensibilities; in almost every area mentioned above these children, by word, action or appearance, manage to give teachers the feeling that they are immoral and not respectable. In terms of physical appearance and condition they disgust and depress the middle-class teacher. Even this young woman, whose emancipation from conventional morality is symbolized in her habitual use of the argot of the jazz musician, was horrified by the absence of the toothbrush from the lives of her lower-class students:

> It's just horribly depressing, you know. I mean, it just gets you down. I'll give you an example. A kid complained of a toothache one day. Well, I thought I could take a look and see if I could help him or something so I told him to open his mouth. I almost wigged when I saw his mouth. His teeth were all rotten, every one of them. Just filthy and rotten. Man, I mean, I was really shocked, you know. I said, 'Don't you have a toothbrush?' He said no, they were only his baby teeth and Ma said he didn't need a toothbrush for that. So I really got upset and looked in all their mouths. Man, I never saw anything like it. They were all like that, practically. I asked how many had toothbrushes, and about a quarter of them had them. Boy, that's terrible. And I don't dig that crap about baby teeth either, because they start getting molars when they're six, I know that. So I gave them a talking to, but what good does it do? The kid's mouth was just rotten. They never heard of a toothbrush or going to a dentist.

These children, too, are more apt than the other groups to be dishonest in some way that will get them into trouble with law enforcement officials. The early (by middle-class standards) sexual maturity of such children is quite upsetting to the teacher:

> One thing about these girls is, well, some of them are not very nice girls. One girl in my class I've had two years now. She makes her money on the side as a prostitute. She's had several children . . . This was a disturbing influence on the rest of the class.

Many teachers reported great shock on finding that words which were innocent to them had obscene meanings for their lower-class students:

> I decided to read them a story one day. I started reading them 'Puss in Boots' and they just burst out laughing. I couldn't understand what I had said that had made them burst out like that. I went back over the story and tried to find out what it might be. I couldn't see anything that would make them laugh. I couldn't see anything at all in the story. Later one of the other teachers asked me what had happened. She was one of the older teachers. I told her that I didn't know; that I was just reading them a story and they thought it was extremely funny. She asked me what story I read them and I told her 'Puss in the Boots.' She said, 'Oh, I should have warned you not to read that one.' It seems that Puss means something else

to them. It means something awful – I wouldn't even tell you what. It doesn't mean a thing to us.[12]

Warner, Havighurst and Loeb note that 'unless the middle-class values change in America, we must expect the influence of the schools to favor the values of material success, individual striving, thrift, and social mobility.'[13] Here again, the 'slum' child violates the teacher's moral sense by failing to display these virtues:

> Many of these children don't realize the worth of an education. They have no desire to improve themselves. And they don't care much about school and schoolwork as a result. That makes it very difficult to teach them.
>   That kind of problem is particularly bad in a school like ――――. That's not a very privileged school. It's very under-privileged, as a matter of fact. So we have a pretty tough element there, a bunch of bums, I might as well say it. That kind you can't teach at all. They don't want to be there at all, and so you can't do anything with them. And even many of the others – they're simply indifferent to the advantages of education. So they're indifferent, they don't care about their homework.

This behavior of the lower-class child is all the more repellent to the teacher because she finds it incomprehensible; she cannot conceive that any normal human being would act in such a way. This teacher stresses the anxiety aroused in the inexperienced teacher by her inability to provide herself with a rational explanation for her pupils' behavior:

> We had one of the girls who just came to the school last year and she used to come and talk to me quite a bit. I know that it was just terrible for her. You know, I don't think she'd ever had anything to do with Negroes before she got there and she was just mystified, didn't know what to do. She was bewildered. She came to me one day almost in tears and said, 'But they don't want to learn, they don't even want to learn. Why is that?' Well, she had me there.

It is worth noting that the behavior of the 'better' children, even when morally unacceptable, is less distressing to the teacher, who feels that, in this case, she can produce a reasonable explanation for the behavior. An example of such an explanation is the following:

> I mean, they're spoiled, you know. A great many of them are only children. Naturally, they're used to having their own way, and they don't like to be told what to do. Well, if a child is in a room that I'm teaching he's going to be told what to do, that's all there is to it. Or if they're not spoiled that way, they're the second child and they never got the affection the first one did, not that their mother didn't love them, but they didn't get as much affection, so they're not so easy to handle either.

IV

We have shown that school teachers experience problems in working with their students to the degree that those students fail to exhibit in reality the qualities of the image of the ideal pupil which teachers hold. In a stratified urban society there are many groups whose life-style and culture produce children who do not meet the standards of this image, and who are thus impossible for teachers like these to work with effectively. Programs of action intended to increase the educational opportunities of the under-privileged in our society should take account of the manner in which teachers interpret and react to the cultural traits of this group, and the institutional consequences of their behavior.[14] Such programs might profitably aim at producing teachers who can cope effectively with the problems of teaching this group and not, by their reactions to class differences, perpetuate the existing inequities.

A more general statement of the findings is now in order. Professionals depend on their environing society to provide them with clients who meet the standards of their image of the ideal client. Social class cultures, among other factors, may operate to produce many clients who, in one way or another, fail to meet these specifications and therefore aggravate one or another of the basic problems of the worker–client relation (three were considered in this paper).

In attacking this problem we touch on one of the basic elements of the relation between institutions and society, for the differences between ideal and reality place in high relief the implicit assumptions which institutions, through their functionaries, make about the society around them. All institutions have embedded in them some set of assumptions about the nature of the society and the individuals with whom they deal, and we must get at these assumptions, and their embodiment in actual social interaction, in order fully to understand these organizations. We can, perhaps, best begin our work on this problem by studying those institutions which, like the school, make assumptions which have high visibility because of their variation from reality.

Notes

1. See Becker (1951a) for further discussion of this point.
2. Warner, Havighurst and Loeb (1944).
3. Hollingshead (1949).
4. Davis (1950).
5. The entire research has been reported in Becker (1951b).
6. Davis (1946), p. 99.
7. Waller (1932), p. 197.
8. Although all service occupations tend to have such problems of control over their clients, the problem is undoubtedly aggravated in situations like the school where those upon whom the service is being performed are not there of their own volition, but rather because of the wishes of some other group (the parents in this case).
9. Davis (1950), pp. 34–5.

10. Wagenschein (1950), pp. 58–9.
11. This is part of the process of job adjustment described in detail in Becker (1952b).
12. Interview by Miriam Wagenschein. The lack of common meanings in this situation symbolizes the great cultural and moral distance between teacher and 'slum' child.
13. Wagenschein (1950), p. 172.
14. One of the important institutional consequences of these class preferences is a constant movement of teachers away from lower-class schools, which prevents these schools from retaining experienced teachers and from maintaining some continuity in teaching and administration.

PART 2

Teachers and Teaching

3 The Teacher in the Authority System of the Public School*

Editor's commentary

In the previous section, we were introduced to Howard Becker's classic study of 60 teachers in the Chicago school system — a study that was used in a range of articles. Having examined the teacher's relationship with her pupils, Becker turns his attention to the teacher's relations with parents, school principals (headteachers) and other teachers. Once again, extensive use is made of the in-depth interviews that were conducted with the Chicago school teachers to examine the teacher's rights, the problems involved in getting others to accept her conception of her rights and the methods used by teachers to handle a diverse range of social groups.

Institutions can be thought of as forms of collective action which are somewhat firmly established.[1] These forms consist of the organized and related activities of several socially defined categories of people. In service institutions (like the school) the major categories of people so defined are those who do the work of the institution, its functionaries, and those for whom the work is done, its clients. These categories are often subdivided, so that there may be several categories of functionaries and several varieties of client.

One aspect of the institutional organization of activity is a division of authority, a set of shared understandings specifying the amount and kind of control each kind of person involved in the institution is to have over others: who is allowed to do what, and who may give orders to whom. This authority is subject to stresses and possible change to the degree that participants ignore the shared understandings and refuse to operate in terms of them. A chronic feature of service institutions is the indifference or ignorance of the client with regard

* This chapter is based on research done under a grant from the Committee on Education, Training and Research in Race Relations of the University of Chicago. Originally published in the *Journal of Educational Sociology* (1953), 27: 128–41.

to the authority system set up by institutional functionaries; this stems from the fact that he looks at the institution's operation from other perspectives and with other interests.[2] In addition to the problems of authority which arise in the internal life of any organization, the service institution's functionaries must deal with such problems in the client relationship as well. One of their preoccupations tends to be the maintenance of their authority definitions over those of clients, in order to assure a stable and congenial work setting.

This paper deals with the authority problems of the metropolitan public school teacher. I have elsewhere described the problems of the teacher in her relations with her pupils,[3] and will here continue that discussion to include the teacher's relations with parents, principals, and other teachers. The following points will be considered in connection with each of these relationships: the teacher's conception of her rights and prerogatives, her problems in getting and maintaining acceptance of this conception on the part of others, and the methods used to handle such problems. The picture one should get is that of the teacher striving to maintain what she regards as her legitimate sphere of authority in the face of possible challenge by others. This analysis of the working authority system of the public school is followed by a discussion which attempts to point up its more general relevance. The description presented here is based on sixty long and detailed interviews with teachers in the Chicago public schools.[4]

Teacher and parent

The teacher conceives of herself as a professional with specialized training and knowledge in the field of her school activity: teaching and taking care of children. To her, the parent is a person who lacks such background and is therefore unable to understand her problems properly. Such a person, as the following quotation shows, is considered to have no legitimate right to interfere with the work of the school in any way:

> One thing, I don't think a parent should try and tell you what to do in your classroom, or interfere in any way with your teaching. I don't think that's right and I would never permit it. After all, I've a special education to fit me to do what I'm doing, and a great many of them have never had any education at all, to speak of, and even if they did, they certainly haven't had my experience. So I would never let a parent interfere with my teaching.

Hers is the legitimate authority in the classroom and the parent should not interfere with it.

Problems of authority appear whenever parents challenge this conception, and are potentially present whenever parents become involved in the school's operation. They become so involved because the teacher attempts to make use of them to bolster her authority over the child, or because they become aware of some event about which they wish to complain. In either case the teacher

fears a possible challenge of her basic assumption that the parent has no legitimate voice with regard to what is done to her child in school.

In the first instance, the teacher may send for the parent to secure her help in
dealing with a 'problem child'. But this is always done with an eye to possible
consequences for her authority. Thus, this expedient is avoided with parents of
higher social-class position, who may not only fail to help solve the problem
but may actually accuse the teacher of being the source of the problem and
defend the child, thus materially weakening the teacher's power over her
children:

> You've got these parents who, you know, they don't think that their
> child could do anything wrong, can't conceive of it. If a teacher has to
> reprimand their child for something they're up in arms right away, it
> couldn't be that the child did anything wrong, it must be the teacher. So
> it's a lot of bother. And the children come from those kind of homes, so
> you can imagine that they're the same way.

The teacher feels more secure with lower-class parents, whom she considers
less likely challengers. But they fail to help solve the problem, either ignoring
the teacher's requests or responding in a way that increases the problem or is
personally distasteful to the teacher.

> [They] have a problem child, but you can't get them to school for love or
> money. You can send notes home, you can write letters, you can call up,
> but they just won't come.
>
> If you send for [the child's] parents, they're liable to beat the child or
> something. I've seen a mother bring an ironing cord to school and beat
> her child with it, right in front of me. And, of course, that's not what you
> want at all.

This tactic, then, is ordinarily dangerous in the sense that the teacher's authority may be undermined by its consequences. Where it is not dangerous, it
tends to be useless for strengthening authority over the child. This reinforces
the notion that the parent has no place in the school.

Parents may also become involved in the school's operation on their own
initiative, when they come to complain about some action of the school's
functionaries. Teachers recognize that there are kinds of activity about which
parents have a legitimate right to complain, for which they may legitimately be
held responsible, although the consequences of the exercise of this right are
greatly feared. They recognize, that is, that the community, in giving them a
mandate to teach, reserves the right to interfere when that mandate is not acted
on in the 'proper' manner. As Cooley put it:

> The rule of public opinion, then, means for the most part a latent auth-
> ority which the public will exercise when sufficiently dissatisfied with the
> specialist who is in charge of a particular function.[5]

Teachers fear that the exercise of this latent authority by parents will be
dangerous to them.

One form of this fear is a fear that one will be held responsible for any physical harm that befalls the child:

> As far as the worst thing that could happen to me here in school, I'd say it would be if something awful happened someplace where I was supposed to be and wasn't. That would be terrible.

This, it is obvious, is more than a concern for the child's welfare. It is also a concern that the teacher not be held responsible for that welfare in such a way as to give the parents cause for complaint, as the following incident makes clear:

> I've never had any trouble like that when the children were in my care. Of course, if it happens on the playground or someplace where I'm not there to watch, then it's not my responsibility, you see . . . My children have had accidents. Last year, two of the little boys got into a fight. They were out on the playground and Ronald gave Nick a little push, you know, and one thing led to another and pretty soon Nick threw a big stone at Ronald and cut the back of his head open. It was terrible to happen, but it wasn't my fault. I wasn't out there when it happened and wasn't supposed to be . . . Now if it had happened in my room when I was in there or should have been in there, that's different, then I would be responsible and I'd have had something to worry about. That's why I'm always careful when there's something like that might happen. For instance, when we have work with scissors I always am on my toes and keep looking over the whole room in case anything should happen like that.

Another area in which a similar fear that the parents will exercise their legitimate latent authority arises is that of teaching competence; the following incident is the kind that provokes such fears:

> There was a French teacher – well, there's no question about it, the old man was senile. He was getting near retirement. I think he was sixty-four and had one year to go to retire. The parents began to complain that he couldn't teach. That was true, of course, he couldn't teach any more. He'd just get up in front of his classes and sort of mumble along. Well, the parents came to school and put so much pressure on that they had to get rid of him.

The teachers' fear in these and similar situations is that intrusion by the parents, even on legitimate grounds, will damage their authority position and make them subject to forms of control that are, for them, illegitimate – control by outsiders. This fear is greatest with higher class groups, who are considered quick to complain and challenge the school's authority. Such parents are regarded as organized and militant and, consequently, dangerous. In the lower-class school, on the other hand:

> We don't have any PTA at all. You see, most of the parents work; in most families it's both parents who work. So that there can't be much of a PTA.

These parents are not likely to interfere.

To illustrate this point, one teacher told a story of one of her pupils stabbing another with a scissors, and contrasted the reaction of the lower-class mother with that to be expected from the parents of higher status whose children she now taught:

> I sure expected the Momma to show up, but she never showed. I guess the Negroes are so used to being squelched that they just take it as a matter of course, you know, and never complain about anything. Momma never showed up at all. You take a neighborhood like the one I'm teaching in now, why, my God, they'd be sueing the Board of Education and me, and there'd be a court trial and everything.

It is because of dangers like this that movement to a school in such a neighborhood, desirable as it might be for other reasons, is feared.[6]

The school is for the teacher, then, a place in which the entrance of the parent on the scene is always potentially dangerous. People faced with chronic potential danger ordinarily develop some means of handling it should it become 'real' rather than 'potential,' some kind of defense. The more elaborate defenses will be considered below. Here I want to point to the existence of devices which teachers develop or grow into which allow them some means of defense in face-to-face interaction with the parent.

These devices operate by building up in the parent's mind an image of herself and of her relation to the teacher which leads her to respect the teacher's authority and subordinate herself to it:

> Quite often the offense is a matter of sassiness or backtalk . . . So I'll explain to the parent, and tell him that the child has been sassy and disrespectful. And I ask them if they would like to be treated like that if they came to a group of children . . . I say, 'Now I can tell just by looking at you, though I've never met you before, that you're not the kind of a person who wants this child to grow up to be disrespectful like that. You want that child to grow up mannerly and polite.' Well, when I put it to them that way, there's never any argument about it . . . Of course, I don't mean that I'm not sincere when I say those things, because I most certainly am. But still, they have that effect on those people.

The danger may also be reduced when the teacher, over a period of years, grows into a kind of relationship with the parents of the community which minimizes the possibilities of conflict and challenge:

> If you have a teacher who's been in a school twenty years, say, why she's known in that community. Like as not she's had some of the parents as pupils. They know her and they are more willing to help her in handling the children than if they didn't know who she was.

If the teacher works in the same neighborhood that she lives in she may acquire a similar advantage, although there is some evidence that the degree of advantage is a function of the teacher's age. Where she is a middle-aged woman whose neighborhood social life is carried on those women of similar age who are the parents of her pupils, the relationship gives her a distinct advantage in dealing with those same women in the school situation. If, however, she is a younger woman, parents are likely to regard her as 'a kid from the neighborhood' and treat her accordingly, and the danger of her authority being successfully challenged is that much greater.

In short, the teacher wishes to avoid any dispute over her authority with parents and feels that this can be accomplished best when the parent does not get involved in the school's operation any more than absolutely necessary. The devices described are used to handle the 'parent problem' when it arises, but none of them are foolproof and every teacher is aware of the everpresent possibility of a parent intruding and endangering her authority. This constant danger creates a need for defenses and the relations of teacher and principal and of teachers to one another are shaped by this need. The internal organization of the school may be seen as a system of defenses against parental intrusion.

Teacher and Principal

The principal is accepted as the supreme authority in the school:

> After all, he's the principal, he is the boss, what he says should go, you know what I mean . . . He's the principal and he's the authority, and you have to follow his orders. That's all there is to it.

This is true no matter how poorly he fills the position. The office contains the authority, which is legitimated in terms of the same principles of professional education and experience which the teacher uses to legitimate her authority over parents.

But this acceptance of superiority has limits. Teachers have a well-developed conception of just how and toward what ends the principal's authority should be used, and conflict arises when it is used without regard for the teachers' expectations. These expectations are especially clear with regard to the teacher's relationships with parents and pupils, where the principal is expected to act to uphold the teacher's authority regardless of circumstances. Failure to do this produces dissatisfaction and conflict, for such action by the principal is considered one of the most efficient defenses against attack on authority, whether from parents or pupils.

The principal is expected to 'back the teacher up' – support her authority – in all cases of parental 'interference.' This is, for teachers, one of the major criteria of a 'good' principal. In this next quotation the teacher reacts to the failure of a principal to provide this:

> That's another thing the teachers have against her. She really can't be counted on to back you up against a child or a parent. She got one of our teachers most irate with her, and I can't say I blame her. The child was being very difficult and it ended up with a conference with the parent,

principal, and teacher. And the principal had the nerve to say to the parent that she couldn't understand the difficulty, none of the other teachers who had the child had ever had any trouble. Well, that was nothing but a damn lie, if you'll excuse me. . . . And everybody knew it was a lie. . . . And the principal knew it too, she must have. And yet she had the nerve to stand there and say that in front of the teacher and the parent. She should never have done that at all, even if it was true she shouldn't have said it. [Interviewer: What was the right thing to do?] Well, naturally, what she should have done is to stand behind the teacher all the way. Otherwise, the teacher loses face with the kids and with the parents and that makes it harder for her to keep order or anything from then on.

This necessity for support is independent of the legitimacy of the teacher's action; she can be punished later, but without parents knowing about it. And the principal should use any means necessary to preserve authority, lying himself or supporting the teacher's lies:

> You could always count on him to back you up. If a parent came to school hollering that a teacher had struck her child, Mr. D—— would handle it. He'd say, 'Why, Mrs. So-an-So, I'm sure you must be mistaken. I can't believe that any of our teachers would do a thing like that. Of course, I'll look into the matter and do what's necessary but I'm sure you've made a mistake. You know how children are.' And he'd go on like that until he had talked them out of the whole thing.
>
> Of course the teacher would certainly catch it later. He'd call them down to the office and really give them a tongue lashing that they wouldn't forget. But he never failed them when it came to parents.

Not all principals live up to this expectation. Their failure to support the teacher is attributed to cowardice, 'liberalism,' or an unfortunate ability to see both sides of a question. The withholding of support may also, however, be a deliberate gesture of disapproval and punishment. This undermining of the teacher's authority is one of the most extreme and effective sanctions at the principal's command:

> [The teacher had started a class project in which the class, boys and girls, made towels to be given to the parents as Christmas presents.] We were quite well along in our project when in walked this principal one day. And did she give it to me! Boy! She wanted to know what the idea was. I told her it was our Christmas project and that I didn't see anything the matter with it. Well, she fussed and fumed. Finally, she said, 'Alright, you may continue. But I warn you if there are any complaints by fathers to the Board downtown about one of our teachers making sissies out of their boys you will have to take the full responsibility for it. I'm not going to take any responsibility for this kind of thing.' And out she marched.

Teachers expect the same kind of support and defense in their dealings with pupils, again without regard for the justice of any particular student complaint.

If the students find the principal a friendly court of appeal, it is much harder for the teacher to maintain control over them.[7]

The amount of threat to authority, in the form of challenges to classroom control, appears to teachers to be directly related to the principal's strictness. Where he fails to act impressively 'tough' the school has a restless atmosphere and control over pupils is difficult to attain. The opposite is true where the children know that the principal will support any action of a teacher.

> The children are scared to death of her [the principal]. All she has to do is walk down the hall and let the children hear her footsteps and right away the children would perk up and get very attentive. They're really afraid of her. But it's better that way than the other.

Such a principal can materially minimize the discipline problem, and is especially prized in the lower-class school, where this problem is greatest.

The principal provides this solid underpinning for the teachers' authority over pupils by daily acts of 'toughness', daily reaffirmations of his intention to keep the children 'in line.' The following quotation contrasts successful and unsuccessful principal activity in this area:

> For instance, let's take a case where a teacher sends a pupil down to the office . . . When you send a child down to this new principal, he goes down there and he sits on the bench there . . . Pretty soon, the clerk needs a messenger and she sees this boy sitting there. Well, she sends him running all over the school. That's no punishment as far as he's concerned. Not at all.
>
>   The old principal didn't do things that way. If a child was sent down to the office he knew he was in for a rough time and he didn't like it much. Mr. G—— would walk out of his office and look over the children sitting on the bench and I mean he'd look right through them, each one of them. You could just see them shiver when he looked at them. Then he'd walk back in the office and they could see him going over papers, writing. Then, he'd send for them, one at a time. And he'd give them a lecture, a real lecture. Then he'd give them some punishment, like writing an essay on good manners and memorizing it so they could come and recite it to him the next day by heart. Well, that was effective. They didn't like being sent to Mr. G——. When you sent someone there that was the end of it. They didn't relish the idea of going there another time. That's the kind of backing up a teacher likes to feel she can count on.

The principal is expected to support all teachers in this way, even the chronic complainers who do not deserve it:

> If the principal's any good he knows that the complaints of a woman like that don't mean anything but he's got to back her just the same. But he knows that when a teacher is down complaining about students twice a week that there's nothing the matter with the students, there's something the matter with her. And he knows that if a teacher comes down once a

semester with a student that the kid has probably committed a real crime, really done something bad. And his punishments will vary accordingly.

The teacher's authority, then, is subject to attack by pupils and may be strengthened or weakened depending on which way the principal throws the weight of his authority. Teachers expect the principal to throw it their way, and provide them with a needed defense.

The need for recognition of their independent professional authority informs teachers' conceptions of the principal's supervisory role. It is legitimate for him to give professional criticism, but only in a way that preserves this professional authority. He should give 'constructive' rather than 'arbitrary' orders, 'ask' rather than 'snoop.' It is the infringement of authority that is the real distinction in these pairs of terms. For example:

> You see, a principal ought to give you good supervision. He ought to go around and visit his teachers and see how they're doing – come and sit in the room awhile and then if he has any constructive criticism to make, speak to the teacher about it privately later. Not this nagging bitching that some of them go in for, you know what I mean, but real constructive criticism.
>
> But I've seen some of those bastards that would go so far as to really bawl someone out in public. Now that's a terrible thing to do. They don't care who it's in front of, either. It might be a parent, or it might be other teachers, or it might even be the kids. That's terrible, but they actually do it.

Conflict arises when the principal ignores his teachers' need for professional independence and defense against attacks on authority. Both principal and teachers command sanctions which may be used to win such a conflict and establish their definition of the situation: i.e., they have available means for controlling each other's behavior. The principal has, as noted above, the powerful weapon of refusing to support the teacher in crucial situations; but this has the drawback of antagonizing other teachers and, also, is not available to a principal whose trouble with teachers stems from his initial failure to do this.

The principal's administrative functions provide him with his most commonly used sanctions. As administrator he allocates extra work of various kinds, equipment, rooms, and (in the elementary school) pupils to his teachers. In each category, some things are desired by teachers while others are disliked – some rooms are better than others, some equipment newer, etc. By distributing the desired things to a given teacher's disadvantage, the principal can effectively discipline her. A subtle use of such sanctions is seen in this statement:

> *Teacher.* That woman really used to run the school, too. You had to do just what she said.
> *Interviewer.* What did she do if you 'disobeyed?'
> *Teacher.* There were lots of things she could do. She had charge of assigning children to their new rooms when they passed. If she didn't

like you she could really make it tough for you. You'd get all the slow children and all the behavior problems the dregs of the school. After six months of that you'd really know what work meant. She had methods like that.

Such sanctions are ineffective against those few teachers who are either eccentric or determined enough to ignore them. They may also fail in lower-class schools where the teacher does not intend to stay.[8]

The sanctions teachers can apply to a principal who respect or protect their authority are somewhat less direct. They may just ignore him: 'After all if the principal gets to be too big a bother, all you have to do is walk in your room and shut the door, and he can't bother you.' Another weapon is hardly a weapon at all – making use of the power to request transfer to another school in the system. It achieves its force when many teachers use it, presumably causing higher authorities to question the principal's ability:

I know of one instance, a principal of that type, practically every teacher in her school asked to leave. Well, you might think that was because of a group that just didn't get along with the new principal. But when three or four sets of teachers go through a school like that, then you know something's wrong.

Finally, the teachers may collectively agree on a line of passive resistance, and just do things their way, without any reference to the principal's desires.

In some cases of extreme conflict, the teachers (some of whom may have been located in the school for a longer period than the principal) may use their connections in the community to create sentiment against the principal. Cooperative action of parents and teachers directed toward the principal's superiors is the teachers' ultimate sanction.

The principal, then, is expected to provide a defense against parental interference and student revolt, by supporting and protecting the teacher whenever her authority is challenged. He is expected, in his supervisory role, to respect the teacher's independence. When he does not do these things a conflict may arise. Both parties to the conflict have at their disposal effective means of controlling the other's behavior, so that the ordinary situation is one of compromise (if there is a dispute at all), with sanctions being used only when the agreed-on boundaries are overstepped.

Colleague relations

It is considered that teachers ought to cooperate to defend themselves against authority attacks and to refrain from directly endangering the authority of another teacher. Teachers, like other work groups, develop a sense that they share a similar position and common dangers, and this provides them with a feeling of colleagueship that makes them amenable to influence in these directions by fellow teachers.

Challenging of another teacher so as to diminish her authority is the basic crime:

> For one thing, you must never question another teacher's grade, no matter if you know it's unjustified. That just wouldn't do. There are some teachers that mark unfairly. A girl, or say a boy, will have a four 'S' report book and this woman will mark it a 'G' . . . Well, I hate to see them get a deal like that, but there's nothing you can do.

Another teacher put it more generally: 'For one thing, no teacher should ever disagree with another teacher or contradict her, in front of a pupil.' The result in terms of authority vis-à-vis students is feared: 'Just let another teacher raise her eyebrow funny, just so they [the children] know, and they don't miss a thing, and their respect for you goes down right away.' With regard to authority threats by parents it is felt that teachers should not try to cast responsibility for actions which may provoke parental interference on another teacher.

Since teachers work in separate rooms and deal with their own groups of parents and pupils, it is hard for another teacher to get the opportunity to break these rules, even if she were so inclined. This difficulty is increased by an informal rule against entering another teacher's room while she is teaching. Breaches of these rules are rare and, when they do occur, are usually a kind of punishment aimed at a colleague disliked for exceeding the group work quotas or for more personal reasons. However, the danger inherent in such an action – that it may affect your own authority in some way or be employed against you – is so feared that it is seldom used.

In short, teachers can depend on each other to 'act right' in authority situations, because of colleague feeling, lack of opportunity to act 'wrong,' and fear of the consequences of such action.

Discussion

I have presented the teacher as a person who is concerned (among other things) with maintaining what she considers to be her legitimate authority over pupils and parents, with avoiding and defending against challenges from these sources. In her view, the principal and other teachers should help her in building a system of defenses against such challenges. Through feelings of colleagueship and the use of various kinds of sanctions, a system of defenses and secrecy (oriented toward preventing the intrusion of parents and children into the authority system) is organized.

This picture discloses certain points of general relevance for the study of institutional authority systems. In the first place, an institution like the school can be seen as a small, self-contained system of social control. Its functionaries (principal and teachers) are able to control one another; each has some power to influence the others' conduct. This creates a stable and predictable work setting, in which the limits of behavior for every individual are known, and in which one can build a satisfactory authority position of which he can be sure, knowing that he has certain methods of controlling those who ignore his authority.

In contrast the activities of those who are outside the professional group are not involved in such a network of mutual understanding and control. Parents do not necessarily share the values by which the teacher legitimates her authority. And while parents can apply sanctions to the teacher, the teacher has no means of control which she can use in return, in direct retaliation.

To the teacher, then, the parent appears as an unpredictable and uncontrollable element, as a force which endangers and may even destroy the existing authority system over which she has some measure of control. For this reason, teachers (and principals who abide by their expectations) carry on an essentially secretive relationship vis-à-vis parents and the community, trying to prevent any event which will give these groups a permanent place of authority in the school situation. The emphasis on never admitting mistakes of school personnel to parents is an attempt to prevent these outsiders (who would not be subject to teacher control) from getting any excuse which might justify their intrusion into and possible destruction of the existing authority system.

This suggests the general proposition that the relations of institutional functionaries to one another are relations of mutual influence and control, and that outsiders are systematically prevented from exerting any authority over the institution's operations because they are not involved in this web of control and would literally be uncontrollable, and destructive of the institutional organization, as the functionaries desire it to be preserved, if they were allowed such authority.[9]

Notes

1. Cf. Hughes (1942).
2. See my earlier statement in Becker (1951a).
3. Becker (1952a).
4. Details of method are reported in Becker (1951b).
5. Cooley (1927), p. 131.
6. Becker (1952b), p. 475.
7. Cf. Wolff (1950), p. 235: 'The position of the subordinate in regard to his subordinate is favourable if the latter, in his turn, is subordinate to a still higher authority in which the former finds support.'
8. See Becker (1952b), pp. 472–3.
9. Cf. Max Weber: 'Bureaucratic administration always tends to be an administration of "secret sessions": in so far as it can, it hides its knowledge and action from criticism . . . the tendency towards secrecy in certain administrative fields follows their material nature: everywhere that the power interests of the domination structure toward *the outside* are at stake . . . we find secrecy.' Gerth and Mills (1946), p. 233.

4 The Career of the Chicago Public School Teacher*

Editor's commentary

One of the key concepts developed within the symbolic interactionist tradition in sociology is that of career. In this classic account of Chicago public school teachers, Howard Becker illustrates how the concept can be creatively used in an empirical study.

Within this chapter, Becker analyses the career movement and career patterns that developed among Chicago school teachers. Once again, the evidence is taken from his empirical study based on in-depth interviews with 60 teachers. On the basis of the data, Becker concludes that there is a horizontal (as opposed to vertical) aspect of career movement among Chicago school teachers. At the end of the article, Becker points the way towards a series of questions that can form the basis of further empirical studies within and beyond the field of education.

In common with much of his work, Becker provides a basis from which other sociologists can develop their studies in conceptual terms.

The concept of *career* has proved of great use in understanding and analyzing the dynamics of work organizations and the movement and fate of individuals within them. The term refers, to paraphrase Hall, to the patterned series of adjustments made by the individual to the 'network of institutions, formal organizations, and informal relationships'[1] in which the work of the occupation is performed. This series of adjustments is typically considered in terms of movement up or down between positions differentiated by their rank in some formal or informal hierarchy of prestige, influence, and income. The literature in the field has devoted itself primarily to an analysis of the types, stages, and contingencies of careers, so conceived, in various occupations.[2] We may refer to such mobility through a hierarchy of ranked positions, if a spatial metaphor be allowed, as the *vertical* aspect of the career.

* This chapter was originally published in the *American Journal of Sociology* (1952), 57: 470–7.

By focusing our attention on this aspect of career movement, we may tend to overlook what might, in contrast, be called the *horizontal* aspect of the career: movement among the positions available at one level of such a hierarchy. We need not assume that occupational positions which share some characteristics because of their similar rank in a formal structure are identical in all respects. They may, in fact, differ widely in the configuration of the occupation's basic problems which they present. That is, all positions at one level of a work hierarchy, while theoretically identical, may not be equally easy or rewarding places in which to work. Given this fact, people tend to move in patterned ways among the possible positions, seeking that situation which affords the most desirable setting in which to meet and grapple with the basic problems of their work. In some occupations more than others, and for some individuals more than others, this kind of career movement assumes greater importance than the vertical variety, sometimes to such an extent that the entire career line consists of movement entirely at one level of a work hierarchy.

The teachers of the Chicago public schools are a group whose careers typically tend toward this latter extreme. Although any educationally qualified teacher can take the examination for the position of principal and attempt ascent through the school system's administrative hierarchy, few make the effort. Most see their careers purely in teaching, in movement among the various schools in the Chicago system.[3] Even those attempting this kind of vertical mobility anticipate a stay of some years in the teacher category and, during that time, see that segment of their career in much the same way. This paper analyzes the nature of this area of career movement among teachers and describes the types of careers found in this group. These, of course, are not the only patterns which we may expect to find in this horizontal plane of career movement. It remains for further research in other occupations to discern other career varieties and conditions under which each type occurs.

The Chicago school system

The positions open to a particular teacher in the system at a given time appear, in general, quite similar, all having about the same prestige, income, and power attached to them. This is not to deny the existence of variations in income created by the operation of seniority rules or of differences in informal power and prestige based on length of service and length of stay in a given school. The fact remains that, for an individual with a given amount of seniority who is about to begin in a school new to her, all teaching positions in the Chicago system are the same with regard to prestige, influence, and income.

Though the available teaching positions in the city schools are similar in formal characteristics, they differ widely in the configuration of the occupation's basic work problems they present. The teacher's career consists of movement among these various schools in search of the most satisfactory position to work in, the position in which the problems are least aggravated and most susceptible of solution. Work problems arise in the teacher's relations with the important categories of people in the structure of the school: children, parents, principal, and other teachers. Her most difficult problems arise in her interaction with her pupils. Teachers feel that the form and degree of the latter problems vary considerably with the social-class background of the students.

Let me summarize the teacher's view of these problems and of their relation to the various social-class groups which might furnish her with students. The interviewees typically distinguished three class groups: (1) a bottom stratum, probably equivalent to the lower-lower and parts of the upper-lower class,[4] and including, for the teacher, all Negroes; (2) and upper stratum, probably equivalent to the upper-middle class; and (3) a middle stratum, probably equivalent to the lower-middle and parts of the upper-lower class. Three major kinds of problems were described as arising in dealings with pupils: (1) the problem of *teaching*, producing some change in the child's skills and knowledge which can be attributed to one's own efforts; (2) the problem of *discipline*, maintaining order and control over the children's activity; and (3) the problem of *moral acceptability*, bringing one's self to bear some traits of the children which one considers immoral and revolting. The teacher believes the lowest group, 'slum' children, difficult to teach, uncontrollable and violent in the sphere of discipline, and morally unacceptable on all scores, from physical cleanliness to the spheres of sex and 'ambition to get ahead.' Children of the upper group, from the 'better neighborhoods,' were felt to be quick learners and easy to teach but somewhat 'spoiled' and difficult to control, and lacking in the important moral traits of politeness and respect for elders. Teachers thought the middle group hard-working but slow to learn, extremely easy to control, and most acceptable on the moral level.

Other important problems arise in interaction with parents, principal, and colleagues and revolve primarily around the issue of authority. Parents of the highest status groups and certain kinds of principals are extremely threatening to the authority the teacher feels basic to the maintenance of her role; in certain situations colleagues, too, may act in such a way as to diminish her authority.

Thus, positions at the teaching level may be very satisfactory or highly undesirable, depending on the presence or absence of the 'right' kind of pupils, parents, principal, and colleagues. Where any of these positions are filled by the 'wrong' kind of person, the teacher feels that she is in an unfavorable situation in which to deal with the important problems of her work. Teachers in schools of this kind are dissatisfied and wish to move to schools where 'working conditions' will be more satisfactory.

Career movement for the Chicago teacher is, in essence, movement from one school to another, some schools being more and others less satisfactory places in which to work. Such movement is accomplished under the Board of Education's rules governing transfer, which allow a teacher, after serving in a position for more than a year, to request transfer to one of as many as ten other positions. Movement to one of these positions is possible when an opening occurs for which there is no applicant whose request is of longer standing, and transfer takes place upon approval by the principal of the new school.

The career patterns found in this social matrix may not be typical of all career movements of this horizontal type. It is likely that their presence will be limited to occupational organizations which, like the Chicago school system, are impersonal and bureaucratic and in which mobility is accomplished primarily through the manipulation of formal procedures.

Career patterns

The greatest problems of work occur in lower-class schools and, consequently, most movement in the system results from dissatisfaction with the social-class composition of these school populations. Movement in the system, then, tends to be out from the 'slums' to the 'better' neighborhoods, primarily because of the characteristics of the pupils. Since there are few or no requests for transfer to 'slum' schools, the need for teachers is filled by the assignment to such schools of teachers beginning careers in the Chicago system. Thus, the new teacher typically begins her career in the least desirable kind of school.[5] From this beginning two major types of careers develop.

The first variety of career is characterized by an immediate attempt to move to a 'better' school in a 'better' neighborhood. The majority of interviewees reporting first assignment to a 'slum' school had already made or were in the process of making such a transfer. The attitude is well put in this quotation:

When you first get assigned you almost naturally get assigned to one of those poorer schools, because those naturally are among the first to have openings because people are always transferring out of them to other schools. Then you go and request to be transferred to other schools nearer your home or in some nicer neighborhood. Naturally the vacancies don't come as quickly in those schools because people want to stay there once they get there. I think that every teacher strives to get into a nicer neighborhood.

Making a successful move of this kind is contingent on several factors. First, one must have fairly precise knowledge as to which schools are 'good' and which are not, so that one may make requests wisely. Without such knowledge, acquired through access to the 'grapevine,' what appears to be a desirable move may prove to be nothing more than a jump from the frying pan into the fire, as the following teacher's experience indicates:

When I put my name down for the ten schools. I put my name down for one school out around ——— ['nice' neighborhood]. I didn't know anything about it, what the principal was like or anything, but it had a short list. Well, I heard later from several people that I had really made a mistake. They had a principal there that was really a terror. She just made it miserable for everyone . . .

But I was telling you about what happened to me. Or almost did. After I had heard about this principal, I heard that she was down one day to observe me. Well, I was really frightened. If she had taken me I would have been out of luck, I would really have had to stay there a year. But she never showed up in my room . . . But, whatever it was, I was certainly happy that I didn't have to go there. It just shows that you have to be careful about what school you pick.

Second, one must not be of an ethnic type or have a personal reputation which will cause the principal to use his power of informal rejection. Though a transferee may be rejected through formal bureaucratic procedure, the principal finds it easier and less embarrassing to get the same result through this method, described by a Negro teacher:

All he's got to do is say, 'I don't think you'll be very happy at our school.' You take the hint. Because if the principal decides you're going to be unhappy, you will be, don't worry. No question about that. He can fix it so that you have every discipline problem in the grade you're teaching right in your room. That's enough to do it right there. So it really doesn't pay to go if you're not wanted. You can fight it if you want, but I'm too old for that kind of thing now.

This destroys the attractive qualities of the school to which transfer was desired and turns choice in a new direction.

Finally, one must be patient enough to wait for the transfer to the 'right' school to be consummated, not succumbing to the temptation to transfer to a less desirable but more accessible school:

When I got assigned to —— [Negro school], for instance, I went right downtown and signed on ten lists in this vicinity. I've lived out here for twenty-five years and I expect to stay here, so I signed for those schools and decided I'd wait ten years if necessary, till I found a vacancy in the vicinity.

The majority of teachers have careers of this type, in which an initial stay in an undesirable 'slum' school is followed by manipulation of the transfer system in such a way as to achieve assignment to a more desirable kind of school.

Thirteen interviewees, however, had careers of a different type, characterized by a permanent adjustment to the 'slum' school situation. These careers resulted from a process of adjustment to the particular work situation which, while operating in all schools, is seen most clearly where it has such a radical effect on the further development of the career, tying the teacher to a school she would otherwise consider undesirable. The process begins when the teacher, for any of a number of possible reasons, remains in the undesirable school for a number of years. During this stay changes take place in her and in her relations with other members of the school's social structure which make this unsatisfactory school an easier place to work in and change her view of the benefits to be gained by transferring elsewhere. Under the appropriate circumstances, a person's entire career may be spent in one such school.

During this initial stay changes take place in the teacher's skills and attitudes which ease the discomfort of teaching at the 'slum' school. First, she learns new teaching and disciplinary techniques which enable her to deal adequately with 'slum' children, although they are not suited for use with other social-class groups:

Technically, you're not supposed to lay a hand on a kid. Well, they don't, technically. But there are a lot of ways of handling a kid so that it doesn't show – and then it's the teacher's word against the kid's so the kid hasn't got a chance. Like dear Mrs. G——. She gets mad at a kid, she takes him out in the hall. She gets him stood up against the wall. Then she's got a way of chucking the kid under the chin, only hard, so that it knocks his head back against the wall. It doesn't leave a mark on him. But when he comes back in that room he can hardly see straight, he's so knocked out.

Further, the teacher revises her expectations about the amount of material she can teach and learns to be satisfied with a smaller accomplishment; a principal of a 'slum' school described such an adjustment on the part of her teachers:

Our teachers are pretty well satisfied if the children can read and do simple number work when they leave here . . . They're just trying to get these basic things over. So that if the children go to high school they'll be able to make some kind of showing and keep their heads above water.

She thus acquires a routine of work which is customary, congenial, and predictable; any change would require a drastic change in deep-seated habits.

Finally, she finds for herself explanations for actions of the children which she has previously found revolting and immoral, and these explanations allow her to 'understand' the behavior of the children as human, rather than as the activity of lunatics or animals:

I finally received my permanent assignment at E——. That's that big colored school. Frankly, I wasn't ready for anything like that. I thought I'd go crazy those first few months I was there. I wasn't used to that kind of restlessness and noise. The room was never really quiet at all. There was always a low undertone, a humming, of conversation, whispering, and shoving . . . I didn't think I would ever be able to stand it. But as I came to understand them, then it seemed different. When I could understand the conditions they were brought up in, the kind of family life and home background that they had, it seemed more natural that they should act that way. And I really kind of got used to it after awhile.

At the same time that these changes are taking place in the teacher's perspectives, she is also gradually being integrated into the network of social relations that make up the school in such a way as to ease the problems associated with the 'slum' school. In the first place, the teacher, during a long stay in a school, comes to be accepted by the other teachers as a trustworthy equal and acquires positions of influence and prestige in the informal colleague structure. These changes make it easier for her to maintain her position of authority vis-à-vis children and principal. Any move from the school would mean a loss of such position and its advantages and the need to win colleague acceptance elsewhere.

Second, the problem of discipline eases when the teacher's reputation for firmness begins to do the work of maintaining order for her: 'I have no trouble with the children. Once you establish a reputation and they know what to expect, they respect you and you have no trouble. Of course, that's different for a new teacher, but when you're established that's no problem at all.'

Finally, problems of maintaining one's authority in relation to parents lessen as one comes to be a 'fixture' in the community and builds up stable and enduring relationships with its families: 'But, as I say, when you've been in that neighborhood as long as I have everyone knows you, and you've been into half their homes, and their's never any trouble at all.'

The 'slum' school is thus, if not ideal, at least bearable and predictable for the teacher who has adjusted to it. She has taken the worst the situation has to offer and has learned to get along with it. She is tied to the school by the routine she has developed to suit its requirements and by the relationships she has built up with others in the school organization. These very adjustments cause her, at the same time, to fear a move to any new school, which would necessitate a rebuilding of these relationships and a complete reorganization of her work techniques and routine. The move to a school in a 'better' neighborhood is particularly feared, desirable as it seems in the abstract, because the teacher used to the relative freedom of the 'slum' school is not sure whether the advantages to be gained in such a move would not be outweighed by the constraint imposed by 'interfering' parents and 'spoiled' children and by the difficulties to be encountered in integrating into a new school structure. This complete adjustment to a particular work situation thus acts as a brake on further mobility through the system.

Career dangers

Either of these career patterns results, finally, in the teacher's achieving a position in which she is more or less settled in a work environment she regards as predictable and satisfactory. Once this occurs, her position and career are subject to dangers occasioned by ecological and administrative events which cause radical changes in the incumbents of important positions in the school structure.

Ecological invasion of a neighborhood produces changes in the social-class group from which pupils and parents of a given school are recruited. This, in turn, changes the nature and intensity of the teacher's work problems and upsets the teacher who has been accustomed to working with a higher status group than the one to which she thus falls heir. The total effect is the destruction of what was once a satisfying place to work in, a position from which no move was intended:

> I've been at this school for about twenty years. It was a lovely school when I first went there . . . Of course, the neighborhood has changed quite a bit since I've been there. It's not what it used to be.

The neighborhood used to be ninety, ninety-five per cent Jewish. Now I don't think there are over forty per cent Jews. The rest are Greek, Italian, a few Irish, it's pretty mixed now. And the children aren't as nice as they used to be.

Ecological and demographic processes may likewise create a change in the age structure of a population which causes a decrease in the number of teachers needed in a particular school and a consequent loss of the position in that school for the person last added to the staff. The effect of neighborhood invasion may be to turn the career in the direction of adjustment to the new group, while the change in local age structure may turn the career back to the earlier phase, in which transfer to a 'nicer' school was sought.

A satisfactory position may also be changed for the worse by a change in principal through transfer or retirement. The departure of a principal may produce changes of such dimension in the school atmosphere as to force teachers to transfer elsewhere. Where the principal has been a major force upholding the teachers' authority in the face of attacks by children and parents, a change can produce a disastrous increase in the problems of discipline and parental interference:

I'm tempted to blame most of it on our new principal . . . [The old principal] kept excellent order. Now the children don't seem to have the same feeling about this man. They're not afraid of him, they don't respect him. And the discipline in the school has suffered tremendously. The whole school is less orderly now.

This problem is considered most serious when the change takes place in a 'slum' school in which the discipline problem has been kept under control primarily through the efforts of a strict principal. Reactions to such an event, and consequent career development, vary in schools in different social-class areas. Such a change in a 'slum' school usually produces an immediate and tremendous increase in teacher turnover. A teacher who had been through such an experience estimated that faculty turnover through transfer rose from almost nothing to 60 per cent or more during the year following the change. Where the change takes place in a 'nicer,' upper-middle-class school, teachers are reluctant to move and give up their hard-won positions, preferring to take a chance on the qualities of the new incumbent. Only if he is particularly unsatisfying are they likely to transfer.

Another fear is that a change in principals will destroy the existing allocation of privilege and influence among the teachers, the new principal failing to respect the informal understandings of the teachers with regard to these matters. The following quotations describe two new principals who acted in this fashion:

He knows what he wants and he does it. Several of the older teachers have tried to explain a few things to him, but he won't have any part of it. Not that they did it in a domineering way or anything, but he just doesn't like that.

He's a good hearted man, he really means well, but he simply doesn't know anything about running a school. He gets all mixed up, listens to people he shouldn't pay any attention to . . . Some people assert themselves and tell him what to do, and he listens to them when he shouldn't.

These statements come from strongly entrenched, 'older' teachers who depend greatly for their power on their influence with the principal. Their dissatisfaction with a new principal seldom affects their careers to the point of causing them to move to another school. On the other hand, the coming of a new principal may be to the great advantage of and ardently desired by younger, less influential teachers. The effect of such an event on the career of a young teacher is illustrated in this quotation:

I was ready to transfer because of the old principal. I just couldn't stand it. But when this new man came in and turned out to be so good. I went downtown and took my name off the transfer list. I want to stay there now . . . Some of those teachers have been there as long as thirty years, you see, and they feel like they really own the place. They want everything done their way. They always had things their way and they were pretty mad when this new principal didn't take to all their ideas.

Any of these events may affect the career, then, in any of several ways, depending on the state of the career at the time the event occurs. The effect of any event must be seen in the context of the type of adjustment made by the individual to the institutional organization in which she works.

Implications

This paper has demonstrated the existence, among Chicago schoolteachers, of a 'horizontal' plane of career strivings and movements and has traced the kind of career patterns which occur, at this level, in a public bureaucracy where movement is achieved through manipulation of formal procedures. It suggests that studies of other occupations, in which greater emphasis on vertical movement may obscure the presence and effects of such horizontal mobility, might well direct their attention to such phenomena.

Further research might also explore in detail the relations between the horizontal mobility discussed here and the vertical mobility more prominent in many occupations. Studies in a number of occupations might give us answers to questions like this: To what extent, and under what circumstances, will a person forego actions which might provide him with a better working situation at one level of an occupational hierarchy in the hope of receiving greater rewards through vertical mobility? Hall notes that those doctors who become members of the influential 'inner fraternity' undergo a 'rigorous system of selection, and a system of prolonged apprenticeship. The participants in the system must be prepared to expect long delays before being rewarded for their loyalty to such a system.'[6] We see that the rewards of eventual acceptance into this important group are attractive enough to keep the fledgling doctor who is apprenticed to it from attempting other ways of bettering his position. Turning the problem around, we may ask to what extent a person will give up possible vertical mobility which might interfere with the successful adjustment he has made in terms of horizontal career movement. A suggestion as to the kinds of relationships and processes to be found here comes from the following statement made by a high-school teacher with regard to mobility within the school system:

> That's one reason why a lot of people aren't interested in taking principal's exams. Suppose they pass and their first assignment is to some school like M—— or T——. And it's likely to be at some low-class colored school like that, because people are always dying to get out of schools like that . . . Those schools are nearly always vacant, so that you have a very good chance of being assigned there when you start in. A lot of people I know will say, 'Why should I leave a nice neighborhood like Morgan Park or South Shore or Hyde Park to go down to a school like that?' . . . These guys figure, 'I should get mixed up with something like that? I like it better where I am.'

Finally, I have explored the phenomenon of adjustment to a particular work situation, the way changes in the individual's perspectives and social relationships acted to tie him to the particular situation and to make it difficult for him to consider movement to another. We may speculate as to the importance and effects of such a process in the vertical mobility prominent in many occupations. One further research problem might be suggested: What are the social mechanisms which function, in occupations where such adjustment is not allowed to remain undisturbed, to bridge the transition between work situations, to break the ties binding the individual to one situation, and to effect a new adjustment elsewhere?

Notes

1. Hall (1948).
2. See Hughes (1937), Hall (1948, 1949) and Dalton (1951).
3. The Chicago system has a high enough salary schedule and sufficient security safeguards to be safe as a system in which a person can make his or her entire career, thus differing from smaller school systems in which teachers do not expect to spend their whole working life.
4. The class categories used in this estimate are those used by Warner and Lunt (1941).
5. Further documentation of this point may be found in Wagenschein (1950) and Winget (1952).
6. Hall (1948).

PART 3

Studies of Socialization

5 The Self and Adult Socialization*

Editor's commentary

Howard Becker has worked predominantly in the theoretical traditions of symbolic interactionism. In this chapter, he examines the concept of self and the meaning attributed to it within symbolic interactionism. In particular, Becker's focus is upon changes in the self after childhood – a process known as 'adult socialization'.

A range of questions are raised throughout the chapter. The main questions include: what situations do socializing agents place their recruits in, and in what ways are these incorporated into the self? What kinds of mechanisms operate to produce changes in adults? Within this chapter Becker makes reference to a range of studies in schools and higher education including his classic study of a medical school with Blanche Geer, Everett Hughes and Anselm Strauss, entitled Boys in White.

Finally, the author examines the concept of commitment that has been widely used by sociologists studying education.

Everyone knows what the self is. It seems to avoid nicely that brace of faults, one or the other of which afflict most concepts of social science. It is not merely a lay term, togged up with a new polysyllabic definition that conceals all the ambiguities of the original, though not very well. Nor is it totally esoteric, a barbarous neologism whose relation to anything known to ordinary men is questionable. (The concept of criminal, as social scientists habitually use it, nicely illustrates the first difficulty. Examples of the second can be found in any sociology textbook.)

The notion of the self avoids these troubles. It is not a term that plays a role in ordinary discourse so that it acquires emotional overtones or gets involved in questions that give rise to argument. On the other hand, it is not totally

* This chapter was originally published in E. Norbeck *et al.* (eds) (1968) *The Study of Personality*, New York: Holt, Rinehart and Winston, pp. 194–208.

foreign. We immediately have an intuitive apprehension of the direction in which the concept points, a general idea of the kind of thing it must be. When a social scientist speaks of the self we feel, with some relief, that for a change we know what he is talking about.

He is talking, of course, about the essential core of the individual, the part that calls itself 'I,' the part that feels, thinks and originates action. Or is he? For despite the seeming clarity of the concept, people do not seem to agree on what they mean by it. This should not be surprising because, in fact, no concept can be defined in isolation. Any concept is, explicitly or implicitly, part of a theoretical system and derives its true meaning from its place in that system, from its relation to the other concepts of which the system is constructed. So the self means one thing in a sociologist's theory and another in a psychologist's, one thing (even among sociological theories) in a structural-functional theory and another in a theory based on symbolic interaction. When we accept the term intuitively we gloss over the differences it hides, differences due to the differing theoretical systems in which it has been embedded. Intuition conceals the disagreement we find when we explore the implications of the word.

In what follows I will approach the concept of self by suggesting the meaning it takes on in the framework of a theory of symbolic interaction, a theory that has long been of major importance in sociology. Of necessity, I will have to say a good deal about the symbolic character of human interaction, the nature of individual action, and the meaning of society before I can begin to speak of the self. But, having done so, I will then be able to proceed directly to the question of changes in the self during the years after childhood, a topic that has in the past few years become popular under the title 'adult socialization.'

Symbolic interaction

The theory of symbolic interaction achieved for a time a commanding position in American sociology. Its dominance arose from the presence of George Herbert Mead at the University of Chicago at the very time that sociology was establishing its first American beachhead there. Mead was a philosopher who developed a theory of society and the self as interdependent parts of the same process, a theory that became internal to the tradition of sociological research that grew up a little later around the figure of Robert E. Park. Mead's theory of symbolic interaction (as it has lately come to be called) provided, with assistance from Dewey and Cooley, the basic imagery sociologists used in their work (Cooley, 1902; Dewey, 1930; Mead, 1934).

Other sources of theoretical support for sociology eventually grew up to dispute the Chicago School. But Mead's theory still seems to me to provide a representation of the character of social life and individual action that is unsurpassed for its fidelity to the nature of society as we experience it (Blumer 1966).

The theory of symbolic interaction takes as its central problem these questions: How is it possible for collective human action to occur? How can people come together in lines of action that mesh with one another in something we can call a collective act? By collective act we should understand not simply cooperative activities, in which people consciously strive to achieve some common goal, but any activity involving two or more people in which individual lines of activity come to have some kind of unity and coherence with one another. In a collective act, to smuggle part of the answer into the definition, individual lines of action are *adjusted* to one another. What I do represents an attempt on my part to come to terms with what you and others have done, to so organize my action that you in turn will be able to respond to it in some meaningful way. Playing a string quartet embodies this notion of mutual adjustment of several individual lines of action. But so do less cooperative activities, such as arguing or fighting, for even in them we mutually take account of what each other does.

By asking how such collective actions are possible, the theory of symbolic interaction marks out a distinctive subject matter and gives a distinctive cast to the study of society. For we may, without exaggeration, regard all of society and its component organizations and institutions as collective acts, as organizations of mutually adjusted lines of individual activity, admittedly of great complexity. A city, a neighborhood, a factory, a church, a family – in each of these many people combine what they do to create a more-or-less recurring pattern of interaction. By focusing on the phenomenon of mutual adjustment, the theory raises two kinds of questions: first, what patterns of mutual adjustment exist, how do they arise and change, and how do they affect the experience of individuals? Second, how is it possible for people to adjust their actions to those of others in such a way as to make collective acts possible? Having raised the question of how collective action is possible, it answers briefly by referring to the phenomenon of mutual adjustment and then asks how that is possible.

The second question concerns us here. Mead, and those who have followed him, explained the mutual adjustment of individual lines of activity by invoking a connected set of conceptions: meaning, symbols, taking the role of the other, society and the self. Actions come to have meaning in a human sense when the person attributes to them the quality of foreshadowing certain other actions that will follow them. The meaning is the as yet uncompleted portion of the total line of activity. Actions become significant symbols when both the actor and those who are interacting with him attribute to them the same meaning. The existence of significant symbols allows the actor to adjust his activities to those of others by anticipating their response to what he does and reorganizing his act so as to take account of what they are likely to do if he does that. What we do when we play chess – think to ourselves, 'If I move here, he'll move there, so I'd better not do that' – is a useful model, although it suggests a more self-conscious process than is ordinarily at work.

The actor, in short, inspects the meaning his action will have for others, assesses its utility in the light of the actions that meaning will provoke in others, and may change the direction of his activity in such a way as to make the anticipated response more nearly what we would like. Each of the actors in a situation does the same. By so doing they arrive at mutually understood symbols and lines of collective action that mesh with one another and thus make society, in the large and in the small, possible. The process of anticipating the response of others in the situation is usually referred to as taking the role of the other.

Our conception of the self arises in this context. Clearly the actions of a person will vary greatly depending on the others whose role he takes. He learns over time from the people he ordinarily associates with certain kinds of meanings to attribute to actions, both his own and theirs. He incorporates into his own activity certain regularized expectations of what his acts will mean, and regularized ways of checking and reorganizing what he does. He takes, in addition to the role of particular others, what Mead referred to as the role of the generalized other, that is, the role of the organization of people in which he is implicated. In Mead's favorite example, the pitcher on a baseball team not only takes into account what the batter is going to do in response to his next pitch, but also what the catcher, the infielders, and outfielders are going to do as well. Similarly, Strauss (1952), has argued that when we use money we are taking into account, as a generalized other, the actions of all those who we know to be involved in handling money and giving monetary value to things: storekeepers, bosses, workers, bankers, and the government.

The self consists, from one point of view, of all the roles we are prepared to take in formulating our own line of action, both the roles of individuals and of generalized others. From another and complementary view, the self is best conceived as a process in which the roles of others are taken and made use of in organizing our own activities. The processual view has the virtue of reminding us that the self is not static, but rather changes as those we interact with change, either by being replaced by others or by themselves acting differently, presumably in response to still other changes in those they interact with.

I have presented a complicated theory in a very summary fashion. The reader who is interested in pursuing it further may be interested in Mead's own writings, admittedly difficult, or may be satisfied with any of a number of good critical accounts already available. (See, for example, McCall and Simmons 1966.)

Adult socialization

The current interest in adult socialization arose out of an attempt to generalize research in a great variety of fields on the changes that take place in people as they move through various institutional settings. Thus, some social psychologists had undertaken studies of the effects of participation in college life on college students; did the participation change them in any way? Others, out of an interest in the professions, had begun to explore the professional training of doctors, lawyers, nurses, and others. Still others, interested in medical sociology and social influences on mental health, had investigated the impact of mental hospitals and other kinds of hospitals on patients. Criminologists concerned themselves with the effects of a stay in prison on convicts, largely from a practical interest in how we might deal with problems of recidivism.

As workers in these different areas strove to find the general rubric under which all these studies might be subsumed and out of which might come propositions that were more abstract and more powerful, they were influenced by a desire common to most sociologists. They wanted to counter the common assumption that the important influences on a person's behavior occur in childhood, that nothing of much importance happens after that, observable changes being merely rearrangements of already existing elements in the personality. Since the term 'socialization' had conventionally been applied to the formation of the personality in childhood, it seemed natural to indicate the belief that all change did not end with adolescence by speaking of 'adult socialization,' thus indicating that the same processes operated throughout the life cycle (Becker and Strauss 1956; Merton, Kendall and Reader 1957; Strauss 1959; Brim and Wheeler 1966).

The process of change indicated by the term can easily, and fruitfully, be conceptualized as a matter of change in the self. Our ways of thinking about our world and acting in it, arising as they do out of the responses of others we have internalized and now use to organize our own behavior prospectively, will change as the others with whom we interact change themselves or are replaced. These changes are precisely the ones students of adult socialization have concerned themselves with, though they have not always used the language of symbolic interaction or the self.

Two central questions have occupied students of adult socialization, each of them generating interesting lines of research and theorizing. The first directs itself outward, into the social context of personal change: What kinds of changes take place under the impact of different kinds of social structures? To put it in somewhat more interactionist terms, and spell out the process involved a little more fully, what kinds of situations do the socializing institutions place their new recruits in, what kinds of responses and expectations do recruits find in those situations, and to what extent and in what ways are these incorporated into the self? The second question, somewhat less studied, turns our attention inward: What kinds of mechanisms operate to produce the changes we observe in adults? I will take these up in order.

Social structure

The study of adult socialization began, naturally enough, with studies of people who were participants in institutions deliberately designed to produce changes in adults. The research was often evaluative in character, designed to find out whether these institutions actually produced the changes they were supposed to produce. Had students of professional schools, at the end of their training, developed the appropriate skills and attitudes? Did prisoners lose their antisocial character and become potentially law-abiding citizens? The studies done usually disappointed the administrators of the institutions studied, for they generally revealed that the desired results were not being achieved. This disappointment led to an inquiry into exactly what was going on, in the hope of discovering how these malfunctions could be avoided. Later inquiries were more complex, went beyond asking simply whether or not the institution achieved its purpose, began to raise more interesting questions, and produced some important discoveries.

One discovery was that the processes of change involved were more complicated than changing in a way that was not officially approved. Wheeler (1961) discovered, for instance, in a study of criminal attitudes among convicts, that their attitudes became more 'antisocial' the longer they were in prison – until the date of their release approached. Then, confronted with the prospect of returning to civilian society, they rapidly shed the criminal orientation that the impact of prison had fostered in them. The curve of 'criminalization,' rather than being a straight line slanting up, was U-shaped. This indicated that one had to take seriously the obvious possibility that the curve of institutional influence might take any of a number of forms, each to be discovered by research rather than being taken for granted.

A second, and equally obvious, discovery was that to speak of 'the institution' as producing change was a vast oversimplification. Institutions do not operate so monolithically. In order to understand the changes that took place one had to look at the structure of the institution in detail – at the particular relationships, both formal and informal, among all the participants, and at the kinds of recurring situations that arose among them. Thus, Stanton and Schwartz (1954) were able to show that mental patients responded dramatically to quarrels that took place between staff members of a mental hospital. A staff member might decide, against the opinion of others, that a particular patient would respond to intensive treatment. The staff member's intramural quarrel would lead him to invest vast amounts of time and effort on the patient and thereby produce radical improvement in the patient. But this investment also drove him out on a limb vis-à-vis his colleagues, and when he discovered his precarious situation, he clambered back to safety. The patient then returned to his original condition or, perhaps, to a worse one.

A third discovery, one that could easily have been predicted from early studies in industrial sociology, was that the people the institution was trying to socialize did not respond to its efforts as individuals, but might, given the opportunity, respond as an organized group. Thus, my colleagues and I, when we studied the socializing effects of a medical school, found it necessary to speak of *student culture* (Becker, Geer, Hughes, and Strauss 1961). By this term we referred to the meanings and understandings generated in interaction among students, the perspectives they developed and acted on in confronting the problems set for them by the school, its authorities, and curriculum. The importance of this observation is that the school's impact does not strike the individual student, with his own unique feelings and emotions, directly. Rather, it is mediated by the interpretations given him by the culture he participates in, a culture which allows him to discount and circumvent some of the efforts of his teachers.

A fourth discovery was that the world beyond the socializing institution played an important part in the socializing process, affecting the amount of impact it had either positively or negatively. This is apparent in the earlier prison example, where the experience of prison actually produced a change in attitudes in a direction opposite to what was desired, this trend being overcome when the prospect of leaving the prison for the larger world loomed ahead. It was, in fact, only during the period when the influence of the outside world was minimized that prison had an influence. Similarly, Davis and Olesen (1963) and their colleagues have shown that the professional training of nurses is deeply marked by the nursing school's inability to shut out external influences, in the form of generalized cultural expectations that the girls will soon marry and never become practicing professionals.

As a consequence of these discoveries and rediscoveries, we can now look at the effects of socializing institutions with something of a model in mind. We know that the changes they produce in the self are likely to be complicated and many-faceted, the course in every case needing to be traced out empirically rather than assumed; we know that we must have detailed knowledge of the pattern of social relations within the socializing organization, as these impinge on the person being changed; we understand that we must see the process of socialization as at least potentially a collective experience, undergone by a group acting in and interpreting their world together, rather than as individuals; and we realize that we cannot ignore the influence of extraorganizational social groups. This gives us a framework for organizing research and a set of central concerns, each of which can be elaborated in specialized investigations.

As an example of the kind of elaboration possible, consider the question of the culture that grows up among those being socialized. (I gave as an example student culture, but it is important to realize that we may similarly have convict culture, patient culture, or a culture of any group confronted with the problem of having attempts made to influence their selves.) Such a culture may or may not develop, depending on the conditions of interaction among those being socialized. In the extreme case, if people cannot communicate they cannot develop a culture (though studies of prisons have shown that people are remarkably ingenious in devising methods of communication in unpromising circumstances). Less extremely, the kind of communication possible and the paths along which it can move will determine the degree and kind of culture that arise (Becker and Geer 1960a).

This leads to analysis of how socializing institutions handle their recruits, as these affect communication possibilities. Wheeler has suggested two dimensions of prime analytic importance (Brim and Wheeler 1966). An institution may take recruits in cohorts, as most schools do when they admit a freshman class each fall, or it may take them in individually, as prisons and hospitals usually do. In the first instance, the recruits will face similar problems simultaneously, which maximizes the need for communication. In the second, each person will face his own problems alone; his fellows will either already have dealt with it and thus no longer be interested or will not be there yet and thus have no awareness of the problem, both tending to make communication more difficult.

The second dimension suggested by Wheeler distinguishes disjunctive from serial forms of socialization. In the first, one cohort or individual is released from the institution before another enters, so that communication is possible only outside the institution's walls; thus, delinquents might tell one another about the juvenile home before they enter it. In the second, several cohorts or individuals are present simultaneously, allowing the culture to be passed on rather than being developed anew, as happens when various perspectives on college life are passed on from one class to the next. Wheeler's analysis explores the consequences for the self of the various combinations of these dimensions that can arise.

Let me conclude our exploration of the effects of social structure by making the essential jump from the socializing institution, which may be taken as an extreme case, to social organizations generally, any of which can be analyzed as though it, in effect, were attempting to socialize its participants. That is, any social organization, of whatever size or complexity, has effects on the selves of those who are involved in its workings. By taking these effects as the object of our attention and viewing every organization, whatever its stated intentions as a socializing organization, we can see how society is perpetually engaged in changing the selves of its members. For every part of society constantly confronts people with new situations and unexpected contingencies, with new others whose role they must take, with new demands and responses to be incorporated into the generalized other. The self, as I remarked earlier, is constantly changing and, in this sense, the label 'adult socialization' is a misnomer, suggesting as it does that the process occurs only occasionally and then only in special places.

Take the processes involved in the use of addictive and intoxicating drugs as an example. Throughout the history of any individual's experience with such drugs, society will confront him with situations that produce appreciable changes in the self. His initial willingness to experiment with drugs that are legally and morally forbidden comes about, typically, after he has begun to participate in circles where drugs are regarded as morally appropriate, as much less dangerous than popularly believed, and as productive of desirable kinds of experience.

When the person first takes any drug, the subjective experience he has will itself be a consequence of the anticipated responses he has learned to expect as a result of his interaction with more experienced users, responses he has incorporated into his self. For example, the novice marihuana user usually experiences nothing at all when he first uses the drug (Becker 1963: 41–58). It is only when other users have pointed out to him subtle variations in how he feels, in how things look and sound to him, that he is willing to credit the drug with having had any effect at all. Similarly, Lindesmith (1947) has shown that people can be habituated to opiate drugs without becoming addicted, so long as no one points out to them the connection between the withdrawal distress they feel and the actual cessation of drug use. It is only when the withdrawal symptoms are interpreted as indicating a need for another shot, an interpretation often furnished by other users, and the shot taken with the predicted relief following, that the process of addiction is set in motion. When a drug-using culture exists, this process operates smoothly. When it does not, as appears to be presently true with respect to LSD-25, people are likely to have a great variety of symptoms, especially anxiety reactions, triggered by their surprise at unexpected effects (because they have not been forecast by participants in such a culture), which may lead to diagnoses of drug-induced psychosis (Becker 1967). Finally, drastic changes in the self may occur as changes in the user's social relations, incident to his drug use, take place. On the one hand, his use may involve him more and more deeply (though it will not necessarily do so) in participation with other users and deviants, whose responses, growing out of a shared culture, will lead him to see himself as one of them and to act more like them and less like any of the other social beings he might be. (This process seems most marked among opiate users, as it is among some homosexuals, and much less marked with users of marihuana.) On the other hand, the use of drugs may bring the person to the attention of authorities (mainly the police) who will brand him as deviant and treat him accordingly, thus inducing a conception of himself as the victim of uninformed outsiders. In either case, he is likely to come out of the process a more confirmed deviant than he entered. (Such processes, of course, do not always run the full course; we particularly need studies of the contingencies of social structure and interaction that lead away from the formation of deviant selves [Becker 1963: 25–39].

To repeat, this extended example serves simply as an instance of the utility of regarding all of society as a socializing mechanism which operates throughout a person's life, creating changes in his self and his behavior. We can just as well view families, occupations, work places, and neighborhoods in this fashion as we can deviant groups and legal authorities. All studies of social organizations of any kind are thus simultaneously studies of adult socialization.

Mechanisms of change

The second major area of research and theorizing in the study of adult socialization, less thoroughly explored than that of social structure, consists of the mechanisms by which participation in social organizations produces change. To introduce the topic, let me first mention that, in the view I have been presenting, stability in the self is taken to be just as problematic as change, so that we shall be looking at mechanisms that operate in both directions.

The general explanations of both stability and change in the self have been hinted at already in the discussion of interactionist theory and require only a slight elaboration. The person, as he participates in social interaction, constantly takes the roles of others, viewing what he does and is about to do from their viewpoint, imputing to his own actions the meanings he anticipates others will impute to them, and appraising the worth of the course on which he has embarked on accordingly. One important implication of this view is that people are not free to act as their inner dispositions (however we may conceptualize them) dictate. Instead, they act as they are constrained to by the actions of their coparticipants. To cite an obvious example, we use grammatical forms and words in accord with how others will understand them, knowing that if we become inventive and make up our own we will not be understood. The example indicates the limits of the proposition: It applies only when the actor wishes to continue interaction and have what he does be intelligible to others, or when he wishes to deceive them in some predictable way. But most social behavior meets this criterion and we need not concern ourselves with those rare instances in which communication is not desired.

The overall mechanism of change in the self, therefore, consists of the continual changes that occur in the person's notions of how others are likely to respond to his actions and the meanings he imputes to his own actions by virtue of the imputations others have made earlier. In his effort to continue interaction, to communicate, the person is continually confronted with his own wrong guesses on this score and thus with the need to revise the roles of others he has incorporated into his self.

This points the way to one specific mechanism of change, which has been called situational adjustment (Becker 1964). As the person moves into a new situation, he discovers that, just because it is new, it contains some unexpected contingencies. Everything does not work out as he expects. People respond to him in unanticipated ways, leading him to appraise what he is doing afresh. He gradually discovers 'how things are done here,' incorporates these new antici-pations of the responses of others into his self and thus adjusts to the situation. He can then continue to act without further change in the self until he is precipitated into a new situation or until the situation changes beneath his feet.

The convicts studied by Wheeler (1961) provide an interesting example of this process. When they first enter prison they are ready to believe that crime does not pay. If it did, would they be there? But they enter an organization which is actually run by other prisoners. While prison administrators make rules and set policy, while guards attempt to enforce those rules and policies, the details of daily life come largely under the surveillance and control of the convicts' shadow government, to which prison officials largely abandon these tasks in return for peace and quiet in the institution. Convict culture is domi-nated by criminal values, by beliefs such as that crime does pay and that one should never snitch on a fellow inmate. To get along with the other prisoners, to play any meaningful part in what goes on and thus influence the conditions of one's own life, it is necessary to act in ways that are congruent with these beliefs and perspectives. Therefore, the longer one is in prison, the more 'criminal' one's perspective.

By the same token, when one is about to leave the prison, it suddenly becomes clear that the world outside is, after all, not the prison and that it does not operate with the criminal perspectives that make collective action possible inside prison walls. The convict realizes that what works inside will probably not work outside, that his adjustment to prison ways will not enable him to interact easily with the people he will meet once he is out. In anticipation of the change in situation, he begins once again to adjust his self, changing it to incorporate the new responses of others he anticipates. (Wheeler did not study what happened to inmates once released. It may well be that the responses of other people include some the prisoners did not anticipate, so that they begin to move once more toward a criminal perspective.)

Situational adjustment is not very complicated, as explanatory mechanisms go. But it seems to explain a great deal of what can be observed of change and stability in the self. The self changes when situations change and remains relatively stable when they do not. Some aspects of the self, however, display great stability over a variety of situational pressures and this easily observable fact points to the need for other explanatory mechanisms. One which is congruent with the position taken here is the mechanism of commitment (Becker 1960).

A person is committed whenever he realizes that it will cost him more to change his line of behavior than it will to continue to act in a way that is consistent with his past actions, and that this state of affairs has come about through some prior action of his own. So committed, he will resist pressures to adjust to new situations that push him in a contrary direction, perhaps moving out of those situations where that is possible or else attempting to change the situation so that he can continue in the direction of his commitment.

A simple example of commitment is a man who is offered a new job but, on calculating its advantages and disadvantages, decides that the cost of taking the new job – in loss of seniority and pension rights, in having to learn a new set of ropes, and so on – makes it prohibitive. The trick in understanding commitment is to grasp the full range of things that have sufficient value to be included in the calculation. In analyzing occupational commitments, Geer (1966) has suggested the following as the minimal list of valuables by which people can be committed: specialized training, which can only be used in the particular occupation; generalized social prestige, which would be lost if one left the occupation; loss of face following an exhibition of being unable to continue at one's chosen work; perquisites of the job to which one has become accustomed; rewarding personal involvements with clients or coworkers; promotional opportunities and other career possibilities; successful situational adjustment to one's present way of doing things; and prestige among colleagues. We can discover how people are committed only by finding out from them which things have sufficient value for their loss to constitute a constraint.

The above list of committing valuables indicates clearly the importance of social structure for the commitment process. Commitment can only occur when there are things present in the environment which are valuable enough that their loss constitutes a real loss. But objects acquire that kind of value only through the operation of a social organization, which both embodies the consensus that ascribes major value to them and creates the structural conditions under which they achieve the necessary attribute of scarcity. If you can get a certain valuable anywhere and with great ease, it is no longer very valuable; but if the social structure makes it scarce, allowing it to be gained in only a few ways that are structurally guarded, it takes on greater value.

Commitment and situational adjustment are clearly of great importance, and each is congruent with a symbolic interactionist approach to the self and adult socialization. Other mechanisms have yet to be discovered and explored. We might speculate, for instance, that involvement will be another such mechanism. People sometimes create a new and at least temporarily stable self by becoming deeply engrossed in a particular activity or group of people, becoming involved in the sense that they no longer take into account the responses of a large number of people with whom they actually interact.

Just as in the case of commitment, one of the crucial questions in the analysis of involvements is how organizations are constructed so as to allow the mechanism to come into play. What kinds of special arrangements allow a person to become so involved in an object, activity, or group that he becomes insensitive to the expectations of others to whom we might equally, on the basis of propinquity and frequency of interaction, expect him to be responsive? Selznick's analysis of the 'fanaticism' of grass roots recruits to the TVA suggests the direction such analyses might take (Selznick, 1953: 210–213). Their fanaticism consisted in always acting with the interests of their local community, and especially its businessmen, in mind, and systematically ignoring the considerations of national interest and bureaucratic constraint put forward by national TVA officials, both in Washington and in the field. They were able to maintain such a consistently one-sided perspective, which caused other agency officials to label them 'fanatics,' because all of their personal interests were bound up in the local community to which they knew they would return. They had no career or other interests in the national agency, so that the arguments and pleas of other officials (which took for granted that everyone had motives like theirs, actually unique to those who did have long term interests in the agency) meant nothing to them.

Generalizing from this case, we can look for the mechanism of involvement to operate whenever people are insulated from the opinions of others who, on the basis of common sense, we would expect to exert influence on them. Those others may be family members, as when an adolescent becomes so involved with his peers that he loses interest in what his parents think about his activities. They may be work associates, as in the TVA case. They may be such community representatives as the police, as when we speak of drug addicts being obsessed or totally involved in the activities surrounding drug use. Or we may have in mind some generalized conception of 'public opinion,' as when we wonder how people can do things that 'everyone knows' are bizarre or unusual, such as being a nudist.

The structural conditions that produce such involvements consist of social arrangements which effectively isolate people from other opinion, which allow them to ignore the expectations of some of those with whom they interact. Physical isolation is the most obvious example: religious sects often attempt to move away from the rest of society, as the Mormons once did, thus protecting their members from the necessity of shaping their behavior in the light of the scandalized responses of others. People may also be isolated, as the grass roots fanatics in TVA were, in an organizational sense; though they interact with others, their organizational positions and interests are so different as to preclude the development of any sense of community or common fate. More subtly, a person may be taught by the members of a group he has joined how to discount the opinions of those he once took seriously. Drug users learn to do this, and so do young people who enter an occupation their parents disapprove.

Or, to conclude this preliminary and incomplete catalogue, they may have an experience commonly defined in one way or another, as setting them apart from others: a serious illness, a religious conversion, an emotional trauma. In every case, the crucial fact is that the person's social relationships – whom he comes into contact with and what they expect of him – become patterned in a way that allows him to dismiss certain categories of people from the self process.

I have briefly indicated the nature of a few mechanisms of change in the self: situational adjustment, through which much of the day-to-day variation in behavior can be explained; commitment, through which the development of long-term interests arises; and involvement, a process of shutting out of potential influences. Much work, empirical and theoretical, remains to be done.

Conclusion

Work in the field of adult socialization has made several contributions to the study of personality. It is one of the developments that is helping to turn the theory of symbolic interaction, by filling it out with research and the differentiated network of propositions research brings with its findings, from a programmatic scheme into a usable scientific tool. By doing this, it also begins to make available to students of personality, by providing the necessary concepts, much of the rich body of data sociologists have accumulated. It has, finally, introduced all of us to some areas of society that had not heretofore been studied and in so doing enriched our understanding both of society and of the great variety of influences which play on the continual development of the self.

6 Personal Change in Adult Life*

Editor's commentary

In the previous chapter in this section Howard Becker introduced us to a series of concepts relating to an analysis of adult socialization within the symbolic interactionist tradition. In this chapter, there is a detailed exploration of two fundamental social processes: situational adjustment and commitment. Once again, Becker draws on his studies of medical students to illustrate the main conceptual themes and the ways in which these concepts can be used by sociologists to examine aspects of social life in schools and higher education.

Personal change in adult life is an important phenomenon deserving more research. In undertaking such research, we should be aware that the kind of change that takes place depends on who is categorizing and evaluating it, and beware of the biases introduced by a too easy acceptance of conventional categories. Instead of seeking explanations of change and stability in elements of personality or in peoples' values, we should look to the effects of social structure on experience. The process of situational adjustment suggests an explanation of change; the process of commitment suggests an explanation of stability.

People often exhibit marked change – in their attitudes, beliefs, behavior and style of interaction – as they move through youth and adulthood. Many social scientists, and others interested in explaining human behavior, think that human beings are governed by deep and relatively unchanging components of the personality or self, so that important changes at late stages in the life cycle are viewed as anomalies that need to be explained away. They may trace the

* A slightly different version of this chapter was presented at the Social Science Research Council Conference on Socialization Through the Life Cycle, New York, May 17, 1963. I wish to thank Orville G. Brim Jr., Blanche Geer, and Anselm L. Strauss for their comments on an earlier draft. Originally published in *Sociometry* (1964), 27: 40–53.

roots of behavior to personality components formed in early childhood – needs, defenses, identifications, and the like – and interpret change in adulthood as simply a variation on an already established theme. Or they may, more sociologically, see the sources of everyday behavior in values established in the society, inculcated in the young during childhood, and maintained thereafter by constraints built into major communal institutions. Like the personality theorists, those who use values as a major explanatory variable see change in adulthood as essentially superficial, a new expression of an unchanging underlying system of values. In either case, the scientist wishes to concern himself with basic processes that will explain lasting trends in individual behavior.

Both these approaches err by taking for granted that the only way we can arrive at generalized explanations of human behavior is by finding some unchanging components in the self or personality. They err as well in making the prior assumption that human beings are essentially unchanging, that changes which affect only such 'superficial' pheneomena as behavior without affecting deeper components of the person are trivial and unimportant.

There are good reasons to deny these assumptions. Brim, for instance, has persuasively argued that there are no 'deep' personality characteristics, traits of character which persist across any and all situations and social roles.[1] In any case, it is clearly a useful strategy to explore the theoretical possibilities opened up by considering what might be true if we look in other directions for generalizeable explanations of human behavior.

A good many studies are now available which suggest that an appropriate area in which further explanations might be sought is that of social structure and its patterned effects on human experience. Two of these seem of special importance, and I devote most of what I have to say to them. The process of *situational adjustment*, in which individuals take on the characteristics required by the situations they participate in, provides an entering wedge into the problem of change. It shows us one example of an explanation which can deal with superficial and immediate changes in behavior and at the same time allow us to make generalized theories about the processes involved. The process of *commitment*, in which externally unrelated interests of the person become linked in such a way as to constrain future behavior, suggests an approach to the problem of personal stability in the face of changing situations. Before dealing with these processes, however, I will consider a problem of definition which reveals a further influence of social structure, this time an influence on the very terms in which problems of socialization are cast.

The eye of the beholder

Many of the changes alleged to take place in adults do not take place at all. Or, rather, a change occurs but an optical illusion causes the outside observer to see it as a change quite different in kind and magnitude from what it really is. The observer (a layman or a social scientist looking at the phenomenon from a layman's point of view), through a semantic transformation, turns an observable change into something quite different.

Take, for example, the commonly asserted proposition that the professional education of physicians stifles their native idealism and turns it into a profound professional cynicism.[2] Educated laymen believe this, and scientific studies have been carried out to test the proposition.[3] Observed changes in the behavior of fledgling physicians attest to its truth. Doctors are in fact inclined to speak with little reverence of the human body; they appear to be and probably are to a large extent unmoved in the emotional way a layman would be by human death; their standards are not as high as the layman thinks they ought to be, their desire for wealth stronger than it ought to be.

People describe these changes with reference to an unanalyzed conception of idealism and cynicism. It would not be unfair to describe the conception as the perspective of a disgruntled patient, who feels that the doctor he has to deal with is thinking about other things than the patient's welfare. The perspective of the disgruntled patient itself draws on some very general lay conceptions which suggest that those who deal with the unpleasant and the unclean – in this case, with death and disease – must of necessity be cynical, since 'normal people' prefer what is pleasant and clean and find the unclean repulsive.

It is typically the case in service occupations, however, that the practitioners who perform the service have a perspective quite different from the clients, patients or customers for whom they perform it.[4] They understand the techniques used by professionals, the reasons for their use in one case and not in another, the contingencies of the work situation and of work careers which affect a man's judgment and behavior, and the occupational ethos and culture which guide him. The client understands nothing of this. In an effort to make sense of his experience with those who serve him, he may resort to the folk notions I have already mentioned, reasoning that people who constantly deal with what decent people avoid may be contaminated: some of the dirt rubs off. The client is never sure that the practitioner has his best interests at heart and tends to suspect the worst.

But why should we assess and evaluate the change that takes place in the doctor as he goes through professional school from the point of view of his patient? Suppose we look at it instead from the characteristic perspective of the medical profession. If we do this, we find (as we would find if we studied the views of almost any occupation toward the institutions which train people for entrance into them) that medical schools are typically regarded as too idealistic. They train students to practice in ways that are not 'practical,' suited to an ideal world but not to the world we live in. They teach students to order more laboratory tests than patients will pay for, to ignore the patient's requests for 'new' drugs or 'popular' treatments,[5] but do not teach students what to do when the waiting room holds more patients than can be seen during one's office hours. Similarly, people often complain of schools of education that they train prospective teachers in techniques that are not adapted to the situation the teacher will really have to deal with; they idealistically assume that the teacher can accomplish ends which in fact cannot be gained in the situations she will face. They do not tell the teacher how to teach a fifteen-year-old fifth grader, nor do they tell her what to do when she discovers a pupil carrying a switch-blade knife.

It is a paradox. In one view, professional training makes physicians less idealistic, in the other, more idealistic. Where does the truth lie? I have already noted that many of the changes seen as signs of increasing cynicism in the young physician do in fact take place. It can equally be demonstrated that the changes which make him seem too idealistic also take place. The medical students we studied at the University of Kansas expected, when they graduated, to practice in ways that would be regarded as hopelessly idealistic by many, if not most, medical practitioners. They proposed to see no more than 20 patients a day; they proposed never to treat a disease without having first made a firm diagnosis. These beliefs, inculcated by a demanding faculty, are just the opposite of the cynicism supposed to afflict the new physician.[6]

The lesson we should learn from this is that personality changes are often present only in the eye of the beholder. Changes do take place in people, but the uninformed outsider interprets the change wrongly. Just as doctors acquire new perspectives and ideas as a result of their medical training, any adult may acquire new perspectives and ideas. But it would be a mistake to assume that these changes represent the kind of fundamental changes suggested by such polar terms as 'idealism' and 'cynicism'. We learn less by studying the students who are alleged to have lost their idealism than we do by studying those who claim they have become cynical.

Even so, adults do change. But we must make sure, not only by our own observation but also by careful analysis of the terms we use to describe what we see, that the changes we try to explain do in fact take place. Parenthetically, an interesting possibility of transferring concepts from the study of adults to the study of socialization of children lies in defining the character of the changes that take place as children develop. Is it too farfetched to say that the definitions ordinarily used are excessively parochial in that they are all arrived at from the adult point of view? What would our theories look like if we made a greater effort to capture the child's point of view? What does he think is happening to him? How does his conception of the process differ from that of the adults who bring him up and those who study his growing up?

Situational adjustment

One of the most common mechanisms in the development of the person in adulthood is the process of situational adjustment. This is a very gross conception, which requires analytic elaboration it has not yet received. But the major outlines are clear. The person, as he moves in and out of a variety of social situations, learns the requirements of continuing in each situation and of success in it. If he has a strong desire to continue, the ability to assess accurately what is required, and can deliver the required performance, the individual turns himself into the kind of person the situation demands.

Broadly considered, this is much the same as Brim's notion of learning adult roles. One learns to be a doctor or a policeman, learns the definitions of the statuses involved and the appropriate behavior with respect to them. But the notion of situational adjustment is more flexible than that of adult role learning. It allows us to deal with smaller units and make a finer analysis. We construct the process of learning an adult role by analyzing sequences of smaller and more numerous situational adjustments. We should have in our minds the picture of a person trying to meet the expectations he encounters in immediate face-to-face situations: doing well in today's chemistry class, managing to be poised and mature on tonight's date, surmounting the small crises of the moment. Sequences and combinations of small units of adjustment produce the larger units of role learning.

If we view situational adjustment as a major process of personal development, we must look to the character of the situation for the explanation of why people change as they do. We ask what there is in the situation that requires the person to act in a certain way or to hold certain beliefs. We do not ask what there is in him that requires the action or belief. All we need to know of the person is that for some reason or another he desires to continue his participation in the situation or to do well in it. From this we can deduce that he will do what he can to do what is necessary in that situation. Our further analysis must adjust itself to the character of the situation.

Thus, for example, in our present study of college undergraduates,[7] we find that they typically share a strong desire to get high grades. Students work very hard to get grades and consider them very important, both for their immediate consequences and as indicators of their own personal ability and worth. We need not look very deeply into the student to see the reason for his emphasis on grades. The social structure of the campus coerces students to believe that grades are important because, in fact, they are important. You cannot join a fraternity or sorority if your grades do not meet a certain minimum standard. You cannot compete for high office in important campus organizations if your grades are not high enough. As many as one-fourth of the students may not be able to remain in school if they do not raise their grades in the next semester. For those who are failing, low grades do not simply mean blocked access to the highest campus honors. Low grades, for these unfortunates, mean that every available moment must be spent studying, that the time the average student spends dating, playing, drinking beer or generally goofing off must be given over to the constant effort to stay in school. Grades are the currency with which the economy of campus social life operates. Only the well-to-do can afford the luxuries: the poor work as hard as they can to eke out a marginal existence.

The perspectives a person acquires as a result of situational adjustments are no more stable than the situation itself or his participation in it. Situations occur in institutions: stable institutions provide stable situations in which little change takes place. When the institutions themselves change, the situations they provide for their participants shift and necessitate development of new patterns of belief and action. When, for instance, a university decides to up-grade its academic program and begins to require more and different kinds of work from its students, they must adjust to the new contingencies with which the change confronts them.

Similarly, if an individual moves in and out of given situations, is a transient rather than a long-term participant, his perspectives will shift with his movement. Wheeler has shown that prisoners become more 'prisonized' the longer they are in prison; they are more likely to make decisions on the basis of criminal than of law-abiding values. But he has also shown that if you analyze prisoners' responses by time still to be served, they become more law-abiding the nearer they approach release.[8] This may be interpreted as a situational shift. The prisoner is frequently sorry that he has been caught and is in a mood to give up crime; he tends to respect law-abiding values. But when he enters prison he enters an institution which, in its lower reaches, is dominated by men wedded to criminal values. Studies of prisons have shown that the most influential prisoners tend to have stable criminal orientations and that inmate society is dominated by these perspectives.[9] In order to 'make out' in the prison, the new inmate discovers that he must make his peace with this criminally oriented social structure, and he does. As he approaches release, however, he realizes that he is going back into a world dominated by people who respect the law and that the criminal values which stand him in such good stead in prison society will not work as well outside. He thereupon begins to shed the criminal values appropriate to the prison and renew his attachment to the law-abiding values of the outside world.

We discovered the same process in the medical school, where students gave up a naive idealistic approach to the problems of medicine for an approach that was specifically oriented toward getting through school. As they approached the end of their schooling, they relinquished their attachment to these school-specific values and once more returned to their concern with problems that would arise in the outer world, albeit with a new and more professional approach than they would have been capable of before.

We find a similar change in college students, when we observe them in the Spring of their last college year. They look back over the four years of school and wonder why they have not spent their time better, wonder if college has been what they wanted. This concern reflects their preoccupation, while in school, with the pursuit of values that are valuable primarily within the confines of the collegiate community: grades, office in campus organizations, and the like. (Even though they justify their pursuit of these ends in part on the basis of their utility in the outside world, students are not sure that the pursuit of other ends, less valued on the campus, might not have even more usefulness for the future.) Now that they are leaving for the adult community, in which other things will be valuable, they find it hard to understand their past concerns as they try, retrospectively, to assess the experience they have just been through.

Situational adjustment is very frequently not an individual process at all, but a collective one. That is, we are not confronted with one person undergoing change, but with an entire cohort, a 'class' of people, who enter the institution and go through its socializing program together. This is most clearly the case in those institutions which typically deal with 'batches' of people.[10] Schools are perhaps the best example, taking in a class of students each year or semester who typically go through the entire training program as a unit, leaving together at the end of their training.

But situational adjustment may have a collective character even where people are not processed in groups. The individual enters the institution alone, or with a small group, but joins a larger group there already, who stand ready to tell him how it is and what he should do, and he will be followed by others for whom he will perform the same good turn.[11] In institutions where people are acted upon in groups by socializing agents, much of the change that takes place – the motivation for it and the perceived desirability of different modes of change – cannot be traced to the predilections of the individual. It is, instead, a function of the interpretive response made by the entire group, the consensus the group reaches with respect to its problems.

The guidelines for our analysis can be found in Sumner's analysis of the development of folkways.[12] A group finds itself sharing a common situation and common problems. Various members of the group experiment with possible solutions to those problems and report their experiences to their fellows. In the course of their collective discussion, the members of the group arrive at a definition of the situation, its problems and possibilities, and develop consensus as to the most appropriate and efficient ways of behaving. This consensus thenceforth constrains the activities of individual members of the group, who will probably act on it, given the opportunity.

The collective character of socialization processes has a profound effect on their consequences. Because the solutions the group reaches have, for the individual being socialized, the character of 'what everyone knows to be true,' he tends to accept them. Random variation in responses that might arise from differences in prior experiences is drastically reduced. Medical students, for instance, began their training with a variety of perspectives on how one ought to approach academic assignments. The pressure generated by their inability to handle the tremendous amount of work given them in the first year anatomy course forced them to adopt collectively one of the many possible solutions to the problem, that of orienting their studying to learning what the faculty was likely to ask about on examinations. (Where the situation does not coerce a completely collective response, variation due to differences in background and experience remains. Irwin and Cressey[13] argue that the behavior of prisoners, both in prison and after release, varies depending on whether the convict was previously a member of the criminal underworld.)

In addition, where the response to problematic situations is collective, members of the group involved develop group loyalties that become part of the environment they must adjust to. Industrial workers are taught by their colleagues to restrict production in order that an entire work group may not be held to the higher production standard one or two people might be able to manage.[14] Medical students, similarly, find that they will only make it harder for others, and eventually for themselves, if they work too hard and 'produce' too much.[15]

One major consequence of the collective character of situational adjustment, a result of the factors just mentioned, is that the group being socialized is able to deviate much more from the standards set by those doing the socializing than would be possible for an individual. Where an individual might feel that his deviant response was idiosyncratic, and thus be open to persuasion to change it, the member of a group knows that there are many who think and act just as he does and is therefore more resistant to pressure and propaganda. A person being socialized alone, likewise, is freer to change his ways than one who is constrained by his loyalties to fellow trainees.

If we use situational adjustment as an explanation for changes in persons during adulthood, the most interesting cases for analysis are the negative cases, those instances in which people do not adjust appropriately to the norms implicit or explicit in the situation. For not everyone adjusts to the kind of major situational forces I have been discussing. Some prison inmates never take on criminal values; some college students fail to adopt campus values and therefore do not put forth their full effort in the pursuit of grades. In large part, cases in which it appears that people are not adjusting to situational pressures are cases in which closer analysis reveals that the situation is actually not the same for everyone involved in the institution. A job in the library may effectively remove the prisoner from the control of more criminally oriented prisoners; *his* situation does not constrain him to adopt criminal values. The political rewards owed a student's living group may require a campus organization to give him an office his grade point average would otherwise make it difficult for him to attain.

More generally, it is often the case that subgroups in an institution will often have somewhat different life situations. College, for instance, is clearly one thing for men, another for women; one thing for members of fraternities and sororities, another for independents. We only rarely find an institution as monolithic as the medical school, in which the environment is, especially during the first two years, exactly alike for everyone. So we must make sure that we have discovered the effective environment of those whose personal development we want to understand.

Even after removing the variation in personal change due to variation in the situation, we will find a few cases in which people sturdily resist situational pressures. Here we can expect to find a corresponding weakness in the desire to remain in the situation or to do well in it, or a determination to remain in the situation only on one's terms or as long as one can get what one wants out of it. Many institutions have enough leeway built into them for a clever and determined operator to survive without much adjustment.

Commitment

The process of situational adjustment allows us to account for the changes people undergo as they move through various situations in their adult life. But we also know that people exhibit some consistency as they move from situation to situation. Their behavior is not infinitely mutable, they are not infinitely flexible. How can we account for the consistency we observe?

Social scientists have increasingly turned to the concept of commitment for an explanation of personal consistency in situations which offer conflicting directives. The term has been used to describe a great variety of social-psychological mechanisms, such a variety that it has no stable meaning. Nevertheless, I think we can isolate at least one process referred to by the term commitment, a process which will help explain a great deal of behavioral consistency.[16]

Briefly, we say a person is committed when we observe him pursuing a consistent line of activity in a sequence of varied situations. Consistent activity persists over time. Further, even though the actor may engage in a variety of disparate acts, he sees them as essentially consistent; from his point of view they serve him in pursuit of the same goal. Finally, it is a distinguishing mark of commitment that the actor rejects other situationally feasible alternatives, choosing from among the available courses of action that which best suits his purpose. In so doing, he often ignores the principle of situational adjustment, pursuing his consistent line of activity in the face of a short-term loss.

The process of commitment consists in the linking of previously extraneous and irrelevant lines of action and sets of rewards to a particular line of action under study. If, for instance, a person refuses to change jobs, even though the new job would offer him a higher salary and better working conditions, we should suspect that his decision is a result of commitment, that other sets of rewards than income and working conditions have become attached to his present job so that it would be too painful for him to change. He may have a large pension at stake, which he will lose if he moves; he may dread the cost of making new friends and learning to get along with new working associates; he may feel that he will get a reputation for being flighty and erratic if he leaves his present job. In each instance, formerly extraneous interests have become linked to keeping his present job. I have elsewhere described this process meta-phorically as the making of side-bets.

> The committed person has acted in such a way as to involve other interests of his, originally extraneous to the action he is engaged in, directly in that action. By his own actions . . . he has staked something of value to him, something originally unrelated to his present line of action, on being consistent in his present behavior. The consequences of inconsistency will be so expensive that inconsistency . . . is no longer a feasible alternative.[17]

A person may make side-bets producing commitments consciously and deliberately or he may acquire them or have them made for him almost without his knowledge, becoming aware that he is committed only when he faces a difficult decision. Side-bets and commitments of the latter type, made by default, arise from the operation of generalized cultural expectations, from the operation of impersonal bureaucratic arrangements, from the process of individual adjustment to social positions, and through the need to save face.

One way of looking at the process of becoming an adult is to view it as a process of gradually acquiring, through the operation of all these mechanisms, a variety of commitments which constrain one to follow a consistent pattern of behavior in many areas of life. Choosing an occupation, getting a job, starting a family – all these may be seen as events which produce lasting commitments and constrain the person's behavior. Careful study might show that the operation of the process of commitment accounts for the well-known fact that juvenile delinquents seldom become adult criminals, but rather turn into respectable, conventional, law-abiding lower-class citizens. It may be that the erratic behavior of the juvenile delinquent is erratic precisely because the boy has not yet taken any actions which commit him more or less permanently to a given line of endeavor.

Viewing commitment as a set of side-bets encourages us to inquire into the kind of currency with which bets are made in the situation under analysis. What things are valuable enough to make side-bets that matter with? What kinds of counters are used in the game under analysis? Very little research has been done on this problem, but I suspect the erratic behavior and 'random' change in adult life result from situations which do not permit people to become committed because they deny to them the means, the chips, with which to make side-bets of any importance.

Members of medical faculties complain, for instance, that students' behavior toward patients is erratic. They do not exhibit the continued interest in or devotion to the patient's welfare supposed to characterize the practicing physician. They leave the hospital at five o'clock, even though a patient assigned to them is in critical condition. Their interest in a surgical patient disappears when the academic schedule sends them to a medical ward and a new set of student duties. The reason for students' lack of interest and devotion becomes clear when we consider their frequent complaint that they are not allowed to exercise medical responsibility, to make crucial decisions or carry out important procedures. Their behavior toward patients can be less constrained than that of a practicing physician precisely because they are never allowed to be in a position where they can make a mistake that matters. No patient's life or welfare depends on them; they need not persist in any particular pattern of activity since deviation costs nothing.[18]

The condition of being unable to make important side-bets and thus commit oneself may be more widespread than we think. Indeed, it may well be that the age at which it becomes possible to make lasting and important side-bets is gradually inching up. People cannot become committed to a consistent line of activity until later in life. As divorce becomes more frequent, for instance, the ability to make a lasting commitment by getting married becomes increasingly rare. In studying the possibilities of commitment afforded by social structures, we discover some of the limits to consistent behavior in adult life.

(It might be useful to apply similar concepts in studies of child socialization. It is likely, for instance, that children can seldom commit themselves. Our society, particularly, does not give them the means with which to make substantial side-bets, nor does it think it appropriate for children to make committing side-bets.

We view childhood and youth as a time when a person can make mistakes that do not count. Therefore, we would expect children's behavior to be flexible and changeable, as in fact it seems to be.)

Situational adjustment and commitment are closely related, but by no means identical, processes. Situational adjustment produces change; the person shifts his behavior with each shift in the situation. Commitment produces stability; the person subordinates immediate situational interests to goals that lie outside the situation. But a stable situation can evoke a well-adjusted pattern of behavior which itself becomes valuable to the person, one of the counters that has meaning in the game he is playing. He can become committed to preserving the adjustment.

We find another such complementary relationship between the two when we consider the length of time one is conventionally expected to spend in a situation, either by oneself or by others, and the degree to which the present situation is seen as having definite connections to important situations anticipated at some later stage of development. If one sees that his present situation is temporary and that later situations will demand something different, the process of adjustment will promote change. If one thinks of the present situation as likely to go on for a long time, he may resist what appear to him temporary situational changes because the strength of the adjustment has committed him to maintaining it. This relationship requires a fuller analysis than I have given it here.

Conclusion

The processes we have considered indicate that social structure creates the conditions for both change and stability in adult life. The structural characteristics of institutions and organizations provide the framework of the situations in which experience dictates the expediency of change. Similarly, they provide the counters with which side-bets can be made and the links between lines of activity out of which commitment grows. Together, they enable us to arrive at general explanations of personal development in adult life without requiring us to posit unvarying characteristics of the person, either elements of personality or of 'value structure.'

A structural explanation of personal change has important implications for attempts to deliberately mold human behavior. In particular, it suggests that we need not try to develop deep and lasting interests, be they values or personality traits, in order to produce the behavior we want. It is enough to create situations which will coerce people into behaving as we want them to and then to create the conditions under which other rewards will become linked to continuing this behavior. A final medical example will make the point. We can agree, perhaps, that surgeons ought not to operate unless there is a real need to do so; the problem of 'unnecessary surgery' has received a great deal of attention both within and outside the medical profession. We might achieve our end by inculcating this rule as a basic value during medical training; or we might use personality tests to select as surgeons only those men whose own needs would lead them to exercise caution. In fact, this problem is approaching solution through a structural innovation: the hospital tissue committee, which examines all tissue removed at surgery and disciplines those surgeons who too frequently remove healthy tissue. Surgeons, whatever their values or personalities, soon learn to be careful when faced with the alternative of exposure or discipline.

Notes

1. Brim (1960), pp. 127–59.
2. This problem is discussed at greater length in Becker and Geer (1958), pp. 50–6, and in Becker *et al.* (1961), pp. 419–33.
3. See Eron (1955), pp. 559–66 and Christie and Merton (1958), Part II, pp. 125-53.
4. See, for a discussion of this point, Becker (1963), pp. 82 ff and Hughes (1958).
5. See Friedson (1961), pp. 200–2.
6. Becker *et al.* (1961), pp. 426–8.
7. Statements about college students are based on preliminary analysis of the data collected in a study of undergraduates at the University of Kansas, in which I collaborated with Blanche Geer and Everett C. Hughes. A monograph reporting our findings is in preparation. The study was supported by the Carnegie Corporation of New York.
8. Wheeler (1961), pp. 697–712.
9. Cressey (1961) and Cloward *et al.* (1960).
10. See Goffman's (1961), use of this idea, pp. 6 and *passim*.
11. See Strauss (1959) and Becker and Strauss (1956), pp. 253–63.
12. Sumner (1907). See also Cohen (1955) and Cloward and Ohlin (1960).
13. Irwin and Cressey (1962). See also Becker and Geer (1960a).
14. Roy (1952).
15. Becker *et al.* (1961), pp. 297–312.
16. Becker (1960).
17. Becker (1960), p. 35.
18. Becker *et al.* (1961), pp. 254–73.

PART 4

Reflections on the
Study of Schooling

7 School is a Lousy Place to Learn Anything In*

Editor's commentary

In this chapter, Howard Becker draws on several of his conceptual and empirical studies to examine the ways in which schools and higher education institutions work. In particular, Becker provides a commentary on teachers, pupils, curricula, testing and evaluation. Altogether, this chapter illustrates the kinds of issues and questions sociologists can examine when studying educational institutions. Finally, Becker suggests ways in which other researchers can explore a series of topics related to education, training, teaching and learning.

Institutions create myths to explain to their participants and the public generally what they do, how they do it, why society needs it done, and how successful they are. Every institution fails in some measure to do the job it promises, and its functionaries find it necessary to explain both that they are trying to do better and that the disparity between promise and performance does not exist, is not serious, or occurs only rarely. Institutional apologias divert our attention from the way the very organization of an institution produces its failures. Further, they divert us from comparisons which might show how others, under a different name and rhetoric, actually perform the institution's characteristic function more effectively.

Schools tell us that people learn in them something they would not otherwise know. Teachers, who know that something, teach it to their pupils. Schools are said to pass the cultural heritage of our society to succeeding generations, both generally in elementary and high school and more differentiatedly in colleges and graduate and professional schools. Finally, while educators readily admit the shortcomings of schools, they do not conceive that anything in the essence of a school might produce those shortcomings or that any other institutional form might do the job better.

* This chapter was originally published in *American Behavioral Scientist* (1972): 85–105.

Though the evidence is both too vast to master and too scanty to allow firm conclusions when the great number and variety of schools is taken into account, it suggests that schools do not achieve the results they set out to achieve. Students do not learn what the school proposes to teach them. Colleges do not make students more liberal and humane (Jacob, 1957: 5), nor do they have any great effect on students' intellectual development and learning (Astin, 1968). Medical school training has little effect on the quality of medicine a doctor practices (Petersen, *et al.*, 1956; Clute, 1963). Actors considered expert by their peers have seldom gone to drama school (Hoffman, n.d.). The spectacle of elementary and secondary education gives credence to Herndon's (1968: 79) wry hypothesis that nobody learns anything in school, but middle-class children learn enough elsewhere to make it appear that schooling is effective; since lower-class children don't learn the material elsewhere, the schools' failure to teach them is apparent.

This brief and selective review of the evidence suggests that educational mythology presents an unrealistic picture of the efficacy of schooling. If schools are ineffective, we can consider how their organization might contribute to that ineffectiveness. Our studies of trade schools and apprenticeships allow us to compare the two and see how the organization of each interferes with doing the job it sets out to do.

The following characterization of how schools work grows out of the continuing comparisons generated by our study of trade schools and on-the-job training situations. The various studies have highlighted one or another dimension of educational organization which I have then applied to conventional schools as well. The comparison suggests structural reasons for the schools' educational failures. By constructing an ideal type, a model of a school at its most school-like, we can understand the dynamics of more mixed cases.

Complex subject matter

We set up a school to teach arithmetic or reading, barbering or beauty culture, when we think the subject matter too complex and difficult to be learned in haphazard ordinary life. The student, we say, must master certain 'basic' conceptions before he can understand the more complicated structures erected on that base; otherwise he will flounder unnecessarily and never really understand the little he learns. Further, he will suffer a confusion that may be emotionally upsetting, even traumatic, and thus compound the difficulties of learning.

The complexity may lie in the subject matter itself. We think it foolish for a person who cannot read to start by attempting written material of the variety and difficulty one might run into in the ordinary world. We give him simplified materials – short words, simple sentences, a small vocabulary. We teach mathematics by starting with simple concepts of number and relation; we think it easier for children to learn 'addition facts' than more abstract conceptions.

The complexity may lie in the social situation the student will later use his knowledge in rather than in the material itself. Techniques of barbering may not be complicated, but we believe a student may have difficulty learning them if he must simultaneously take into account the possible reactions of customers whose hair he has butchered in a beginner-like way. So we set up our school in a way that minimizes the student's anxiety. Barber colleges recruit customers by providing cheap haircuts. Anyone who pays $.75 for a haircut forfeits his right to complain; if he wants a $3.00 haircut, he knows where he can get it, and so does the student barber, who masters his anxiety over complaints by writing his customers off as skid row winos or cheapskates. Similarly, teachers in the barber school Woods studied made it their business to tidy up particularly bad jobs done by students. (Medical schools use similar mechanisms.)

Curriculum

In principle, a curriculum could be tailor-made for each student; the complexities of the subject could be simplified to achieve the uniquely best way for him to learn. In practice, schools develop standardized curricula. They arrange the material in some order of increasing complexity, an order usually thought of as the 'natural' or 'normal' way to approach the subject. They decide what minimum amount of knowledge will be acceptable. They decide on a schedule, time periods in which the student is to learn particular batches of material. They produce, in short, a curriculum, which rests on a conception, usually uninspected, of a normal student who can do that much work and grasp that much material in the time allotted. The eleven-week quarter and the fifteen-week semester are common examples. Anyone who could learn the material more efficiently if it were presented in a different order will have difficulty, as will anyone who needs more or less time than allotted.

Schools could teach students individually, and occasionally make provision to do so. More typically, they process students in batches, treating them as if each were the prototypical normal student for whom they constructed the curriculum. Being part of such a batch naturally constrains the student to behave, as best he can, as though he were prototypical; it is the easiest way to fit into the collective activity he is part of.

Teachers

The curriculum necessarily differs substantially from what competent practitioners of the skill or art in question know how to do, for they do not divide what they know into more and less basic components and seldom see any particular order in which what they know should be presented to a learner. Furthermore, competent practitioners in a subject matter area know only by accident, if at all, the skills of teaching. The inability of competent practitioners to teach planned curricula arises equally with such general topics as arithmetic or reading and with specialized skills like cutting and setting hair or driving an automobile. I may be a proficient user of mathematics and a skilled driver and unable to teach a child either one. Ordinary practitioners in a particular subject, finally, have other things to do than teach beginners, and are ordinarily not available for instructional tasks.

So schools require teachers whose principal work is to teach the planned curriculum to batches of normal students. While teachers want to do their work in the easiest, least troublesome way, they also wish to demonstrate to themselves and others that their work produces results. Do a teacher's pupils know something, when he finishes the standard curriculum, that they did not know before, something worth knowing, something attributable to his efforts? Is it a true grasp of the material such that the student can use it in everyday life? Can he read well enough to get about in a literacy-demanding society? Does he know the craft skills (of welding, nursing, hair-cutting, teaching, writing, or whatever) well enough to work adequately with professional peers? Has he mastered the liberal arts well enough to use the knowledge and sensibility they provide to enrich his private life and inform his public activities?

Teachers assume that the student is as inferior in knowledge as he usually is in age (Geer, 1968). They assume that what they know, the student needs to know. They may want to take his opinions into account, but they do not propose to let him decide which portions of the curriculum he will learn. They insist on having the upper hand in the relationship, searching for ways to augment and solidify control when it is disputed.

Because the teacher devotes his full-time effort to teaching, his own knowledge of what actual situations require may be faulty. This is especially obvious in trade schools, where the trade may change substantially after the teacher leaves it, but it occurs in varying degrees in more academic schools as well. Uncertainty about the teacher's knowledge aggravates problems of control and deepens everyone's sense that school training may not be adequate and may require some checking.

Pupils

Teachers necessarily have pupils. The relationship might be interesting if pupils had more power over its dimensions and content, but the major say on those matters, by common consent of both parties, belongs to the teacher. Students typically (though not always) concede that the teacher knows more about the subject they want to learn than they do; if he did not, there would be little point in studying with him. (Students may refuse to concede the teacher's superiority when they attend school, as they often do, for some purpose other than learning: to avoid being charged as a truant, to secure a draft exemption, or to meet a legal requirement for some other desired activity.) They want to learn and expect that the teacher will help them, even though his activities seem to have no immediate or discernible relation to that goal. When they lose faith in his authority, they refuse to accept the standard curriculum, and the teacher's job becomes more difficult; he must persuade or coerce students into doing what he thinks best.

Students want to know whether they have learned something as they proceed through the curriculum. Their desire may reflect an uncertainty of the
curriculum itself, but more likely reflects a concern with their own abilities.
They think a normal student should be able to learn what the curriculum
proposes in the time allotted. Are they normal? Have they learned what they
should? Do they just think they learned it, while in truth they missed the point
or are doing it the wrong way?

They ask themselves these questions because the school often fails to tell
them whether their understanding is correct, their skill adequate. They need
the answers to see whether their allocation of time and effort needs change and
to confront deeper questions about the suitability of what they have attempted.
Is this the right course for me? The right school? Do I want to spend any more
of my life in pursuits like this? These questions arise for graduate students,
students in professional schools, and students in trade schools equally, though
trade school students have made a lesser commitment and can more easily take
remedial action if they decide they have made a mistake.

Tests and evaluations

The setting in which teachers teach and students learn will be quite different, of
necessity and by design, from the world in which students use what they have
learned. The materials taught differ from the fully complex materials the world
contains. When the student completes the work the school lays out for him,
neither he nor his teacher can be sure there are not crucial differences between
what he has been taught and what will later be required of him. So teachers –
who want to know how their students will fare when they leave school –
students – who wonder whether they are truly prepared for the tasks they will
now have to do – and the rest of the world – which wonders what it can expect
of the graduates – combine their desires for a working knowledge of what is
being accomplished in a demand for tests and other evaluative procedures. A
formal program of evaluation tells teachers they are doing their job compe-
tently, students that they have learned what they came for, and employers,
parents, legislators, and others that the school is doing what is expected of it.

The chief problem in testing students and evaluating their performance is to
concoct tests isomorphic to the real world situations in which the student will
exercise his skills. How do we test whether a student can successfully cut the
hair of a fussy, middle-class executive who worries about his looks, when the
only material available for him to demonstrate his skill on is a sixty-year-old
drunk who falls asleep in the chair and whom both student and instructor
know cannot and will not complain? Beauty colleges solve this problem (as
does the state barber board in conducting licensing examinations) by requiring
the examinee to provide his own subject (usually a relative or friend); medical
schools do not let students perform important or dangerous procedures without supervision by more experienced, licensed physicians. Neither solution is
fully effective, since each avoids some of the most cogent difficulties in social

relationships. But both represent a high in isomorphism between school and practice compared to the written examinations and problem-solving exercises graduate schools, to take a notorious example, habitually use. These more typical examinations differ in gross ways from the tasks examinees will later be called on to do. It is commonplace, but true, to suggest that such tests mainly measure the ability to take tests.

We seldom argue that conventional tests measure the actual skills students are supposed to have learned. Rather, we believe that the test, while not a direct measure, is nevertheless highly correlated with the ability to exercise those skills, though the mechanism by which the alleged correlation occurs is seldom investigated or demonstrated. Common observation suggests the belief is unfounded; we seldom find hard evidence of such correlations. Instead, we rely on test results for want of anything better. In any event, the skills required to perform well on school examinations may not be the same skills required to perform adequately in the situations the school trains people for.

Another difficulty in addition to the divergence between test and real life, is that tests are usually taken at the convenience of the tester, at a time set by the periodicity of the normal curriculum, at the end of the quarter, semester, or year, when the designated material has been covered. The test thus does not measure a student's ultimate knowledge, but his knowledge as of the time of the examination. This feature, among others, increases the student's anxiety, so that the conventional test in some part measures not knowledge, but the student's ability to withstand or cope with anxiety (Mechanic, 1962).

School rewards and student culture

Schools seldom use evaluations of students' performances in an advisory way, to help the student discover areas of weakness which can be strengthened by a changed allocation of effort. Instead, they incorporate the results of such evaluations – grades will do as the generic term – into permanent records, on whose basis people and institutions make decisions bearing on students' futures. Schools vary in the degree to which they allow examination results to become fateful beyond their immediate academic relevance. If grades have fateful consequences, students find it necessary to orient their efforts toward getting good ones; if tests are not isomorphic to the situations in which the abilities being tested will be used, students will have to divert time and effort from what the school wants to teach to what is needed for a good grade. This untoward consequence occurs only when tests do not measure and require the knowledge the school wishes to teach. When the two are the same, the school's reward system evokes exactly the learning teachers desire.

We found an extreme example of the constraint grading and evaluation exercised on student's allocations of their efforts in our study of a college (Becker et al., 1968). Students' grade point averages, being the chief measure available and presumably reasonably accurate, fair, and comparable, affected most other rewards a student might want (or not want to be denied) during and after college. For example, college rules specified a minimum grade point average for initiation into a fraternity or sorority, for holding major office in campus organizations, and for staying in school and graduating. Grades also affected a student's chances of getting into professional or graduate school, as well as the kind of job he might get on graduation. Grades even affected his social life: he might find it harder to meet eligible girls if he did not belong to a fraternity or could not participate in extracurricular activities because of low grades; girls were often reluctant to get involved with anyone who might flunk out. Since whatever a student wanted had to be paid for in high grades, few students felt they could safely avoid learning what was needed for tests. It is hard to say what the desired outcomes of a college's educational efforts are. But if they are a change in values and the acquisition of certain intellectual skills, students might be diverted from such goals by the necessity of studying for exams not requiring those abilities. When what tests require differs from what the school wants to teach and when the school rewards good test performance heavily the structure of the school will systematically divert student effort. In this sense, and to the degree that these conditions are met, schools are structurally self-defeating. Where students have the opportunity to interact and develop collective conceptions of their situation and how it ought to be handled, they may develop a student culture which amplifies and extends this effect. When students agree they must do certain things to give a good performance for evaluation, and when that information is passed on to new students, each student need not experience the disparity and the constraint himself. He knows beforehand, in the way any functioning culture allows us to know, what is coming and how to deal with it. A student culture which advises grade-getting as an optimal strategy decreases the likelihood that students will attempt other strategies, though it does not make that impossible.

Since some students do learn some things that schools want to teach, the above analysis deals with the extreme case. Where some of the conditions outlined above do not obtain, schools will be more successful than the analysis suggests.

On-the-job training

The chief alternative to learning things in school is to learn them on the job, especially if we define on-the-job training broadly. So defined, it includes not only the conventional apprenticeship in a trade, but all the casual learning that goes on in the course of everyday living, the kind of learning Goodman (1968) and Holt (1967) have called to our attention as the way children learn to talk and most other things. Think of living your daily life as a job to give the notion its full meaning. Though I speak mainly of occupational training, keep the larger relevances in mind.

The apprentice learns on the job, in the place where people do in a routine way whatever members of his trade do. He finds himself surrounded from the outset by the characteristic sights, sounds, situations, activities, and problems he will face as long as he remains in the trade (if we reasonably assume the trade does not change in the short run). The butcher's apprentice works in a meat market, where journeymen break down carcasses, cut them into conventionally defined pieces of meat, trim them, price them, and package them. The apprentice ironworker works on a building under construction, where journeymen place beams and girders, rivet and weld them together, place rods for reinforced concrete, do finishing work, and take dangerous walks on narrow beams in high places. (Similarly, the small child, learning to talk, lives in a world in which most of the kinds of talk that go on, simple and complex, go on around him in person, on the radio, or on television; Goodman, 1968). Thus, the learner sees the kind of work he is to learn in all its tangled complexity from the first day, instead of being introduced to those complexities a step at a time in a carefully constructed curriculum. He suffers whatever traumas may arise from realizing all there is to learn. Some apprentices give up their ambitions quickly when they realize what they have gotten into, but those who remain have a pretty good idea of what they are in for from the start. They see the technical difficulties, and dangers, the social complications that may arise with employers and customers, and even the informal requirements of making it with one's work peers.

One consequence follows the immediate accessibility of the full round of activities characteristic of an apprentice's trade. He can participate in these activities right away or on any idiosyncratic schedule he can work out with his fellow workers. No one can learn everything at once, but no principle or rule prevents the apprentice from learning a little of this today, a little of that tomorrow, things in some order no one ever thought of before, or learning to the point where he wants to stop and then switching to something else. He need not, when he wants to learn a certain procedure, wait until its time in a prearranged schedule; nor need he learn something he is not ready for, thinks uninteresting, frightening, or unnecessary. The learner makes his own curriculum.

Teachers

This curriculum is created with the aid of people who know more than he does, who must be persuaded to assist him, or at least not to interfere with his own efforts. Because the learning situation is the real work world – an actual meat market or construction site – no one functions as an official teacher. Everyone has his own job to do, his own set of occupational constraints and rewards. The apprentice does not have a teacher's time and attention guaranteed to him as does a pupil in a conventional school.

This leaves the actual training to the apprentice's own initiative. Competent practitioners will teach him if he can persuade them to, and actual training is thus in some part a function of such formally extraneous traits as the degree of his aggressiveness. A pushy punk learns more than a quiet young man. An ideology common among journeymen suggests that if an apprentice is any good, he will make you teach him: if he does not push, he probably does not have what it takes. This differs diametrically from a conventional school in which learning occurs at the teacher's initiative: you move on when the teacher thinks you are ready.

In such a system, no one rests his self-esteem, reputation, or claim to having done a decent day's work on the amount his students learn. While everyone cares in general that the apprentices eventually learn their trade, no particular person can be blamed or has it on his conscience if any particular apprentice or group of apprentices fails to learn. Teaching is no one's job in particular, so it is no one's fault if no learning occurs.

Two consequences follow from the failure to assign teaching responsibility. On the one hand, when teaching does occur, it is not overlaid with the teacher's own worries about how he is doing; teacher and apprentice can concentrate on the learner's difficulties. Where the teacher has no responsibility, he cannot misuse or fail to meet it. On the other hand, an apprentice may not be taught anything, since he may not be aggressive enough to force anyone to teach him.

External constraints

The characteristic virtues of each kind of learning situation breed characteristic difficulties and vices. Schools divorce themselves from the problems of the everyday world in an effort to make learning easier. They thus create a need for evaluative mechanisms and thus divert student effort from learning to efforts to be evaluated more highly. On-the-job training, in and of the everyday world, provides a realistic and individualized learning setting. But it does that at the cost of making teaching and learning vulnerable to potent external constraints.

The chief constraint arises from setting the educational encounter in a real-life enterprise which has its own problems and imperatives. Meat markets have, as their main purpose, to profitably sell meat to customers. Ironworkers work for a company whose main business is to construct a building or a bridge. Interns (who also undergo a kind of on-the-job training) work in hospitals whose main business is to treat illness (Miller, 1970). Each enterprise requires potential learners and teachers alike to contribute what they can to the success of the enterprise as the price of continued participation.

But the required contribution may prevent teaching or learning. Potential teachers may not have time for it, because of the press of more important business. When journeymen butchers prepare for a steak sale, they do not have time to teach apprentices. When senior physicians handle medical emergencies, they have no time to teach interns. Opportunities for on-the-job learning vary inversely with the amount of work the enterprise must turn out.

Similarly, the apprentice's labor and time may have to do necessary work for the total enterprise that no one else wants to do. An apprentice ironworker's first jobs are fire watch (looking for possible fires set by sparks from welding and riveting operations) and getting coffee for the journeymen. These jobs are not entirely uneducational – going for coffee prepares the novice to 'run the iron' – but apprentices do them not for that reason but because people want them done and the apprentice, lowest man on the totem pole, gets the honor. Apprentice meatcutters start out running the wrapping machine, which packages, seals, and labels the meat. The wrapping machine requires no skill, and working on it falls to the one who cannot do anything else; the work may familiarize the novice with the various cuts of meat, but is not a big step in becoming a butcher. An apprentice may run the wrapping machine for the three years in a large meat department solely because the other workmen, knowing more, can be profitably used elsewhere. Marshall saw one apprentice work on the wrapping machine for three months until a new apprentice was hired; then apprentice 1 was taught new skills while apprentice 2 ran the wrapping machine. No further new apprentice was hired, and apprentice 2 continued to run the wrapping machine. Someone had to. The first apprentice received superior training by the accident of being hired three months earlier and thus being advantageously placed with respect to the needs of the total enterprise.

Another external constraint limiting the opportunity to learn lies in the potential cost – to fellow workers, employers, customers, or the public – of allowing an unskilled apprentice to undertake some task. Because teaching hospitals may be held liable for the damage done a patient, they limit what medical students can do to patients in furthering their own learning. Ironworkers do not allow apprentices to do things that might jeopardize the safety of fellow workers. Meat cutters give apprentices more practice cutting up meat in markets that serve poor populations. The cost of mistakes made on cheap cuts of pork can more easily be absorbed than mistakes made on the expensive steaks sold in markets in more well-to-do neighborhoods.

Some of the things a novice ought to learn (or would like to learn) may occur infrequently during his period of training. A school would make some provision to cover this material, so that the student's competence would not depend on the accidents of history. Medical schools compromise, necessarily, on this point; they systematically *teach* about various diseases, but whether a student has clinical experience with those diseases is left to the chance of whether a patient with a certain disease appears during the student's tenure.

Gross effects of the external environment on the learning situation result from changes in the economy. A depression (or the memory of one, in some trades) may cause journeymen to fear the competition of too many qualified workmen. In consequence, they systematically withhold training and keep apprentices at the classic apprenticeship tasks of sweeping the shop and running out for coffee. Boom times make it harder to get prospective trainees; with more work to be done, apprentices must quickly be pushed into more responsible positions; if they feel ill-used, they may quit, and the enterprise needs their labor to meet its commitments. Under these circumstances, a trainee may be taught thoroughly and rapidly.

In short, what one can learn on the job and who will teach it depend on contingencies unrelated to education or training. The learning situation exists to do some quite different job and is subject to the constraints emanating from the external world, any of which may interfere directly in the novice's training. Many of these interferences have nothing whatever to do with any attribute of the novice, neither his skill nor aptitude, nor his aggressiveness and initiative. The defect is structural.

Evaluation

Even if people who learn on the job never take formal examinations, they do not escape evaluation, which occurs continuously as they go about their daily business. Everything they do is what people in that line of work do, and everyone in a position to observe their performance can immediately see whether they have done it satisfactorily. No person with special training need be present to make the evaluation; most people on the scene can do it. The evaluators not only know the work the novice attempts, but are the very people the novice must please to be successful. On-the-job training thus avoids completely any disparity between what the school tests and what the real world requires. Because the evaluators are part of that real world and what they require is the test, the two are the same.

Facing the process of evaluation in the midst of the work setting has interesting consequences:

1. The learner can take his tests any time he feels ready. Every novice will want to test himself or allow himself to be tested to convince both others and himself that he has mastered some important skill. In schools, tests can be taken only at stated intervals, when the tester gives them; often the student must take them at the time they are given or suffer a serious penalty. Since the on-the-job trainee's test will consist of doing something that could be done every day (or almost every day, allowing for weekly or seasonal variations in the workloads), he can take it at his discretion, simply by announcing that he thinks he can do a particular task. Someone will give him the chance, and both novice and observer can see the result. The test is self-scoring and self-interpreting, since the product either does or does not pass muster in the same way the world usually evaluates it.
2. Because the test consists of performing some routine task, an apprentice can take it repeatedly, without having to wait for any special time, until he finally performs successfully. Unlike the typical school, in which scores are averaged over some time period, only the last test counts. Since the test can be repeated, and since the learner takes the test when he feels ready, he feels less anxiety than over a conventional school test. The results are less fateful.
3. Because his progress is immediately observable, the learner can make a good or bad reputation among the people he will be working with once he has become a full-fledged member of the group. The possibility can cause considerable anxiety. School typically shelters the student from having his bad mistakes known to the people he will eventually join, but mistakes made on the job are fully seen by those people. Further, while school does not let really serious mistakes occur (because it simplifies the curriculum in

ways making that impossible), learning on the job allows costly, even fatal, mistakes to occur, because the actual work cannot be successfully sealed off. An apprentice meatcutter can ruin an expensive side of beef; an apprentice ironworker can unintentionally cripple or kill another worker. In each case, that reputation may dog the perpetrator for years, especially if he harms a valued colleague (Forsyth and Kolenda, 1966: 132).

4. Testing on the job is not restricted to technical material. It includes all the relevant human relations skills as well. Haas provides a detailed example in his analysis of 'binging.' Ironworkers must demonstrate their ability to participate adequately in this earthy teasing before those already established accept them as trustworthy. Schools do not test these skills; on-the-job situations invariably do.

5. Because the testing occurs so much at the insistence of the novice, and because he may not wish to be tested in all or even in very many areas, a person who learns on the job may never be tested on a great variety of matters. In so far as testing has value for either the learner or those who have to work with him or use his services, that value may well be lost. (This is another way of saying that the apprentice may not be taught more than a few of the trade's characteristic skills.)

Relations to the world of work

Educators, as I have already suggested, construct a standard curriculum which includes what they regard as the essential elements anyone must learn to be certified as knowing particular subjects, or as fit to occupy a particular social or occupational position. As we have seen, learning on the job in no way assures that any student will learn such a common core of knowledge. In this, learning on the job realistically reflects the character of most jobs and occupations.

Hughes (1951) has suggested that any job or occupation, any named kind of work, actually consists of a bundle of tasks. Some of those tasks may be taken to be symbolic of the whole, as when we think of courtroom pleading as the definitive legal task. Ordinarily, no single member of the occupation does the full range of tasks associated with it. Differentiation and specialization, characterize most kinds of work, so that a member of the occupation may actually do only one or two tasks from the bundle. A school requires students to learn the entire bundle, in case they are called on to perform any of them, but on-the-job training allows a student to learn, at a minimum, only one, while still becoming a full-fledged member of the trade. On-the-job training thus reflects realistically the demands of the labor market, operating on the assumption that, if a person can get a job doing one of the tasks in the bundle, he knows enough to be an acceptable member of the trade.

Ironworkers present an interesting example of this phenomenon. The characteristic and symbolic act that marks the 'real ironworker' is 'running the iron,' working high above the ground while standing on a four- to eight-inch steel beam. Running the iron takes more nerve than some recruits have, but their failure either to take that test or, if they try, to pass it, does not mean that they cannot be ironworkers. They can do one of the other jobs, requiring more brawn than nerve, such as placing rods for reinforced concrete construction. They will not get the considerable glory that goes with doing the tasks that require bravery, but they can still be ironworkers.

The work world, in short, accommodates what people can do. Apprenticeship and job training prepare people for such a world. They avoid a recruit's difficulties with some portion of the standard curriculum, at the cost of producing a member of the trade who knows less than the complete body of knowledge that might be expected of him.

Conclusions

I have been discussing ideal types. Real-life educational situations usually contain some mixture of school and on-the-job styles of teaching and learning. Thus, medical schools, beauty schools, and barber colleges are schools, but with strong on-the-job emphases. On the other hand, meatcutters and ironworkers may take classes in some subjects. Ordinarily, when we are anxious to teach people something, we remove teaching from the job and organize a school. The above analysis has as its chief implication that schools are lousy places to learn, precisely because we establish them without considering the circumstances under which other ways of proceeding, perhaps less organized, might be more efficient, more humane, or both. Another equally important implication is that on-the-job training is often no better, for the same reason. The analysis has in general been pessimistic, making it appear impossible for anyone to learn anything. Since people do learn, the analysis is clearly insufficient, and I would like to end by considering how this learning occurs.

I do not suggest that students learn *nothing* in school, only that they typically learn what the school does not intend to teach and do much less well with what the school focuses on. We found an excellent example of this in our study of college students. Students learned effective methods of operating politically on campus. But in academic subjects they devoted themselves to getting good grades, a time-consuming activity that presumably accounts for the lack of attitude change Jacob reports and the lack of effect on academic achievement Astin uncovered. The explanation is that they learned their politics on the job, by acting in the political arena of the campus. Imagine what would happen if someone gave a course in 'Operating on Campus,' complete with texts, tests, and grades. Students busy learning how to pass the tests, would never become the effective politicians campus political life produces.

People learn, in spite of the obstacles our analysis suggests, because the schools and job situations in which they learn seldom approach the extreme conditions of these ideal analytic types. Schools are effective, when and where they are, because tests sometimes require what teachers want students to learn, because teachers do not always connect a multitude of other rewards to academic performance, because students are sometimes incapable of developing a culture which maintains and spreads counterfaculty perspectives. On-the-job training is often effective because someone does have time to do a little teaching because the enterprise allows enough leeway for the apprentices to make some mistakes without costing others too much because the things that can interfere with his learning are fortuitous occurrences rather than structural necessities.

On-the-job training, then, for all the difficulties I have mentioned is more likely to produce educational successes, nevertheless I do not propose that we immediately convert all education to an apprenticeship model. Substantial difficulties are associated with that model. Students may be denied the teaching they want, due to the exigencies and constraints of the real-life situation in which the training occurs. Students may learn very little of what we would like to see them know, even though they will probably learn a little something.

Nor is it easy to set up apprenticelike training situations. It requires the specification of educational goals in a more exact way than is common in schools. When schools state 'educational objectives,' they generally content themselves with pious generalities. If you want to create an on-the-job training situation, you must go much farther and find a place in the everyday world where people ordinarily act just as you wish your trainees to act, where the very skills, attitudes, and sensibilities you wish to inculcate are embodied in the daily activities of people trainees will be allowed to associate with. It is often difficult to find a place which wishes to be used as a site for an educational enterprise.

In addition, we sometimes cannot specify our objectives clearly. We may believe that we are training people for an unknown future. We do not know what we want them to know, because we cannot specify the problems and situations they will have to cope with. This may be because the situations that lie ahead of them are too complicated for us to deal with in detail or because we believe the world is going to change so much that we cannot forecast how things will be and thus what a person will need to know to act effectively. Given such a diagnosis, we generally settle for inculcating proper orientations from which students will be able to deduce correct lines of action in specific circumstances, general skills which can be used in a variety of situations, and an ability to learn new material as it becomes available.

We will always have schools, because we will often find ourselves in the dilemma of preparing people for unknown futures. A minimum use of the present analysis might then be to broaden educators' perspectives so that they will be aware of the possibilities of apprenticelike training that may be available to them (Beck and Becker, 1969) and not engage unnecessarily in activities that actively defeat the very ends they seek. Such irrationality can only perpetuate the troubles our schools are already in and deepen the mistrust so many people have of them.

8 Studying Urban Schools*

Editor's commentary

All the chapters in this volume draw on empirical data that have been collected and analysed using ethnographic methods – an approach used in social anthropology and sociology. While many educational studies use this approach, it has not always been widely accepted given the predominance of surveys and quantitative evidence.

As qualitative data have become more widely used in recent years, many social and educational researchers have begun to explore the problems and processes associated with ethnographic studies. In this chapter, Howard Becker adds to this genre by reflecting on the main characteristics of educational ethnography. In particular, he examines the main methods of investigation that are used by ethnographers.

Overall, Becker highlights the problems involved in conducting ethnographic studies in education and highlights those issues that have yet to be resolved.

People have been studying schools and education ethnographically for a long time. Anthropologists, following the lead of Margaret Mead and others, have made the socialization of children into a culture a major concern, and what happened to children in contemporary Western schools could be seen as an example of that process. Sociologists likewise long have been interested in schools. In fact, Willard Waller's classic, *The Sociology of Teaching*, is probably the first ethnography of a contemporary American school.

Waller was not very careful about his methods. He had not really done ethnography so much as he had been the classic participant-as-observer,

* This chapter is a slightly revised version of an invited address presented at the 'Ethnography in Education Research' Forum, Graduate School of Education, University of Pennsylvania, March 1983. The author reflects on the reasons that ethnographic studies are, and probably will continue to be, suspect in the field of education. Appreciation is expressed to Francis A.J. Ianni for help in preparing this paper. Originally published in *Anthropology and Education Quarterly* (1983) 14: 99–108.

making the best of his job as schoolteacher by noting the interesting phenomena occurring around him. But his work had one hallmark of good ethnography. He saw and reported a fact, central to the institution he was
observing, the existence of which no one there would admit: He said that
children did not want to go to school and that adults forced them to, so that
the natural state of social relations in the school was conflict. That seems
obviously true, today as then, and yet the people who take that statement and
its implications seriously (e.g., the writings of Holt or Herndon) still create
controversy. Waller did work of the kind Erving Goffman, in his posthumous
presidential address to the American Sociological Association ('The Interaction Order,' *American Sociological Review*, 48), specified as the proper mode
of sociological inquiry:

> unsponsored analyses of the social arrangements enjoyed by those with
> institutional authority – priests, psychiatrists, school teachers, police, gen-
> erals, government leaders, parents, males, whites, nationals, media oper-
> ators, and all the other well-placed persons who are in a position to give
> official imprint to versions of reality (p. 17).

In many ways, that aspect of Waller's work, and its reception and use, relates
to a problem I want to focus on here. Ethnographic studies of schools, and
perhaps especially of urban schools, have a paradoxical quality. On the one
hand, the ethnographic study of schools has a long and honorable pedigree.
Waller published his book in 1932, and work in the tradition has never stop-
ped. Community studies usually pay attention to schools and education, and
many researchers have spent years in close unfettered observation in schools.
On the other hand, ethnographic studies of schools always have been suspect in
the field of education, if not in the fields of anthropology and sociology in
which the tradition originated. Ethnographic studies have been suspect even
though they frequently produce results the face validity of which is apparent,
and even though they do not have the obvious flaws of other styles of research
common in schools.

Suspicion toward ethnography shows up in many ways. The most obvious –
at least the way it most often comes to my attention – is the defensive posture
of people in education who do such work. They are not neurotically and
unrealistically defensive, either; they are defensive because they are always
being attacked. Ethnographers of education do not receive the professional
courtesy that allows unavoidable and irremediable flaws in one's methods to go
unchallenged. Every version of research on schools has such problems, yet most
of it gets done. But examining committees approve experimental research
designs with well-known but conventionally accepted flaws, while balking at
students' proposals to do ethnographic research. So I get a lot of phone calls
from students and young faculty in education who are looking for legitimation
for what they want to do; I'm sure that most people in the field get similar calls
all the time. Our flaws have to be accounted for and justified every time –
unless we meet among ourselves, and even then much of our attention is
devoted to the attacks we will face when we get home.

Why should ethnographic research in education produce good results and still have such a bad reputation? This paradox has two major causes. One is the way scientific research in education came to be used to justify the failures and discriminatory results of the operation of educational institutions. The other is the inability of ethnographic research to be useful, in that or any other way, to educational practitioners.

Anthropology isn't psychology

Education, as a field of professional scholarly activity and as a public institution, was captured early by the field of psychology. The premise was that education consisted of putting information and skills into the heads of children and other ignorant people. It thus needed a science of learning and, secondarily, of teaching (as opposed, for instance, to a science of school organizations or educational situations). The science that could provide the knowledge on which to base methods of teaching was psychology, the science of the inside of people's heads. This coincided with psychology's decisive turn toward scientism, experimental modes of thought and procedure, and quantification. I'm not familiar enough with the history of psychology to know why this happened, or how and when it did, but it certainly happened. And education people, looking for theories and methods to justify a 'professional' approach to their own work, found everything they needed there.

We all know what followed. First came the enormous growth and success of the testing industry, which quickly assumed authority in areas of major educational concern. Psychological scientists devised tests, some allegedly measuring native ability, others allegedly measuring achievement. As a further consequence, scientific students of the process and institutions of education began their never-ending discoveries of 'how best to' do whatever someone who ran schools and similar institutions thought ought to be done. They discovered, for instance, how best to teach children to read. The only thing wrong with these discoveries was the rapidity with which they were replaced by new, contradictory discoveries. In this, education resembled the entire field of child development on which it has always been parasitical. As we all know from our own experiences as children, if not as parents, child development is the field that for decades alternately has advised everyone, on the basis of good scientific evidence, to feed their babies on demand or on a schedule.

Why did the institutions and leaders of education accept the authority of such a patently fallible group of authorities? I want to develop a hypothesis here, although I have not done the work required to verify it. Briefly, the idea is that increasingly over the decades institutions of education found themselves in a situation in which they had to prove that they were being fair, in the face of substantial and obvious evidence that they were not. In that situation, quantitative scientific psychology provided the required proof. I'll begin the argument by noting that education's swoon into the arms of quantitative scientific psychology coincided with the broad democratization of public education. State and federal governments began to believe that every child was entitled to an education provided free of charge by the state and that every child was capable of profiting from such an education.

I accept the first of those propositions philosophically, and I believe that the second one is empirically true, but contingent. Every child *can* learn what an education is supposed to give, but not all children can learn it taught in the same way, nor can they all learn it on the same schedule. The routinization of education that came with its growth as an industry – its development of standardized methods to be applied *en masse* to batches of students (to hark back to another theme of Erving Goffman's) – meant that everyone who came to school had to be equipped physically, mentally, culturally, and in every other way not just to learn but to learn something presented in just *one* of the many ways it might have been presented. People who could have learned something taught in 'way X' are out of luck if it is only taught in 'way Y' in their school. Similarly, someone who could have learned a body of material in 15 weeks may fail if it comes in a 10-week package.

(The latter point sticks in my mind because of my daughter's experience some years ago, when she switched from San Francisco State College [as it was then known] to the University of California at Berkeley. She reported that, while the courses in calculus in both places covered the same material from the same book, the Berkeley class covered it in 10 weeks while State took 15. I will leave it as an elementary exercise for the reader to work out the arguments by which Berkeley faculty might then have 'proved' that this difference made Berkeley a better school. Anyone who wants extra credit also can assess the logical basis and adequacy of those arguments.)

If an institution purports to do a job uniformly over an entire population, basing its claim for financial and other support on the successful doing of that job, and then fails to do it, the people responsible for the institution (and thus for its failures) have some explaining to do. Suppose public health officials had guaranteed to wipe out an epidemic disease like polio by following a procedure of universal inoculation. Suppose, further, that they succeeded in wiping it out in that portion of the population with the highest income, but that rates, while coming down some, were still high in poorer classes. In so far as they had guaranteed universal results, they would have a big public relations problem.

The proponents of public health might have explained their failure by some characteristic of the people they had not been able to protect – a genetic flaw, perhaps, which made a vaccine not work. That is just what educators did. Rather than ask why their methods did not work universally, as they had claimed, they 'found' that certain measurable characteristics of students accounted for their ability to learn. As for the others – well, either you have it or you don't, and they just don't have it. Too bad! I am, of course, caricaturing a complex matter here and making unnecessarily cruel fun of serious and well-intentioned people. Or . . . is that really the gist of that argument?

Whatever the fairness of my caricature, educators did have a problem. They had promised the moon but could not deliver it. It might have been better not to promise the moon, but they were stuck with that. So, as the saying goes, they blamed the victim. But many people will not accept that diagnosis, most of all the representatives of the people who have been characterized as wanting. How can you persuade skeptics to accept your diagnosis? That is where the scientific psychology of the 1920s and beyond becomes useful. Almost everyone accepts, as a practical matter, what seem patently obvious facts of everyday life, no more than common sense: some people are smarter than others and that is why some people fail in school and others don't.

But how can we tell who is smarter and who is dumber, so that we can see if that is true? More to the point, how – if we are running a school system – can we make those distinctions in such a way that no one can complain that we are being unfair? This brings us to the heart of my speculation. If we are in perpetual danger of being accused of favoritism, discrimination, or racism, we need to be able to show skeptics, legislators, friends, and enemies, that we reached our conclusions by a method that is fair and defensible. We cannot explain that we are promoting Dick and Jane because they come from good families and are keeping Tom and Harriet back because they don't; not in the America we live in, even if that is the reason, and even if there are plenty of countries in which that explanation might be acceptable.

Which methods are fair and impartial? Bitter experience has shown that almost any method that leaves discretion in the hands of the people using it can be misused in a discriminatory way. Any method that lets a judge's 'subjective' judgments come into play may produce a quite improper result, improper in the sense of being offensive to the standards we want to uphold – a discriminatory result instead of a fair one. (I am not talking here about the results of fair methods that produce the results discrimination might have, e.g., the racial segregation produced by a 'color-blind' sorting on economic variables.)

So everyone agrees that 'objective' methods are better. Objective methods seem most clearly objective when they are quantitative, when the judge seems to be doing no more than laying down a ruler alongside something and noting where it falls on the ruler's scale; no room for subjective discrimination in that, or not much. If there is unfairness, it is built into the procedure. It is part of the ruler, and that is where it has to be looked for, the way Allison Davis and others looked for it and found it in the construction of intelligence tests. But those discoveries don't have what is called 'face validity,' and are much less convincing than the obvious parallels between test results and common observation. Kids who test dumb usually look and act dumb in school. That their dumbness may be the result of deep cultural differences between what they know and feel comfortable doing and what the schools require doesn't alter that.

Let me remind you of two well-known cases. Murray and Rosalie Wax and Robert Dumont reported, in their 1964 monograph *Formal Education in an American Indian Community*, that the Native American children who tested dumb, and who also looked and acted stupid in reservation schools, were responding to a setting that systematically devalued what they did know (including the Sioux language) so that they could not display their abilities. They resented it and acted accordingly. Similarly, Jane Mercer reported in *Labeling the Mentally Retarded* (and here I simplify some complex relationships) that mental retardation was a disease children got by going to school. Before they started school, others might (or might not) think them a little slow to catch on to things, but they could perform adequately. When they got to school, however, and were tested, school personnel 'discovered' their retardation. Since these children almost always were from groups whose culture differed significantly from that of the school (Hispanic or black), they had the usual problems and looked dumb enough to make the diagnosis seem reasonable.

Because so many children's troubles with schools are based on cultural differences of this kind, the schools are in a particularly difficult position. The children they fail with are often members of political minorities of whom the schools are specially wary. Courts and legislatures alike may want to catch them discriminating. They don't want to be caught doing that. On the other hand, other constituencies want to prevent what they define as 'reverse discrimination.'

The schools cannot win. What they *can* do is use methods that they can claim are scientific so that the troubles that arise will be visited on someone else. In other words, objective, quantitative, scientific research provides educators with defensible explanations for their failure to deliver on the various and contradictory promises of educators. That prejudices the entire education establishment in favor of such research and against anything else, especially against qualitative research that relies on the sensitivities and seemingly unrestrained judgments of individual researchers.

Ethnographic research therefore runs afoul of a deeply held belief, one embedded in the operations of major institutions. I don't mean to accuse educators of venality. I don't think they say, 'Hey, if we let people do this kind of research it will spoil our explanation of why we can't do the job.' But I do think that reasons like that are part of what lies behind the religious zeal with which people in the education industry espouse quantitative research. That zeal, in turn, helps account for their difficulties with, and complaints about, ethnography.

Anthropology studies (and judges) everybody

Thus, educators, responsible for the successes and failures of educational institutions, understandably mistrust ethnographic studies that provide no rationale for the institution's failure to produce acceptable results with lower class students. Worse yet, ethnographic research, with its emphasis on understanding social organizations as wholes, makes it impossible to confine research to uncovering the shortcomings of students. If you study schools by giving students tests, you may find out that the students have not learned what they are supposed to, but you will be studying the teachers and administrators only indirectly. Ethnographers, however, routinely study *everyone* connected with the school. Most ethnographers of schools have had to deal with the surprise (and sometimes shock) of teachers and administrators who discover that the ethnographers aren't just going to look at the students or subordinate members of the organization, but regard everyone in it, from top to bottom, as fair game for investigation. 'You mean you are going to study us?' That immediately, and always, opens up for them the possibility that we are somehow going to find out that 'it' (whatever 'it' is) is their fault. They may not know what 'it' is, but they can usually see that someone who hangs around long enough, nosing into everything, is bound to find *something* that is their fault. If we insist on sitting in their offices and observing them at work, and not just observing students, we may find out some things they'd rather we didn't.

In fact, we will *always and necessarily* find out those things. Institutions, in the voices of those who lead them and thus are responsible for them to the rest of the world, always lie about how well they do their jobs. 'Lie' is a strong word; the people involved probably prefer to think of what I am talking about as statements of goals that somehow turned out not to be as easy to achieve as they had hoped. But people who don't quite live up to their goals year after year perhaps ought to be more cautious, so I'll stick with 'lie.'

Ethnographers – who hang around forever – are going to see the reality behind the statements of intention. Worse yet, they are going to see that the reality is no accident but is built into the fabric of the organization. Administrators and others involved in an institution do not mind the discovery of 'a few bad apples in the barrel.' (That is the usual phrasing in complaints about studies of police departments.) But they do mind the conclusion that the barrel makes good apples into rotten ones, and that is what ethnographers always are discovering and saying.

In fact, all research on schools has overtones of evaluation. We can't help that. Even if we don't intend our work to be evaluative, the people we study will take it that way, for the good reason that everyone else does and will hold them responsible for whatever we find out that anyone thinks untoward. The quotation from Goffman cited earlier attests to that. It is hard for any of us to avoid making those grossly evaluative judgments ourselves. When we thus 'expose' the inadequacies of one level of an organization, the people at the higher levels don't mind, as long as the results don't suggest that it was *their* fault. Even ethnographies draw boundaries around organizations, leaving some things out of the field of what is to be studied. So long as we leave the higher-ups out, they won't mind a little ethnography. But eventually we almost always get them into the picture and, if we don't, someone else will look at what we have found, take the logical step, and do research at the next higher level. The investigations of the My Lai massacre are a case in point.

Studying higher-ups leads to some funny confrontations that make clear the difference between scientific organization and the bureaucratic hierarchy and self-protectiveness of schools. Years ago, two researchers produced a book that described sociologically the operations of a well-regarded educational program. They had done their research in the town where their university was located. When the book was published and the school principal saw it, he called the chairman of their department and asked, angrily, 'Do you let your people publish stuff like this?'

Anthropology is no help

Beginning in the 1960s educators lost some of their autonomy, some of their control over their institutions. The giant sums that came to them as a part of the national effort to raise the educational levels of poor people, and especially poor blacks, carried some conditions. The most important for my argument is that the schools got no blank checks. They had to produce results, and it would not do to blame the children for failure. That was exactly why they were getting the new money: to discover or create new ways of teaching that would be successful with children for whom the old ways had failed. The shift from an emphasis on learning – what made learning hard for children – changed to an emphasis on programs and what about programs made them fail to produce the promised results.

Conventional evaluations might say you had failed to do the job, but could not tell you, except in the most indirect and tortured way, what caused the failure. People at various levels of the educational establishment worried about this in different ways. Those who handed out money for experiments that were supposed to produce startling new results worried about being cheated and wondered whether the experiments were being carried out as promised. If there were results, did they come from the new methods that were being touted as producing them, or were they an artifact of the selection of those exposed to the new methods? Were the experimenters 'creaming' the population, attributing to new methods results that were really due to the superior ability of those who took part in the experiment? If so, such chicanery proved hard to document. School administrators and educational researchers are skilled manipulators of records. So it seemed like a good idea to observe these programs closely, and to have the observations made by people who were not part of the educational enterprise. Such people might be more 'objective,' even though they didn't use objective methods.

From another direction, many school people sincerely wanted to do a better job for students with whom they hitherto had failed. They understood and accepted all the liberal arguments. What they needed were new methods that worked. Many of them distrusted 'objective' scientific research that evaluated them and found them wanting or that produced yet another in the long list of 'innovations' that soon proved no better than those of their predecessors. Conventional psychologically-oriented testing research could not help them, they were convinced, and they saw hope in the 'depth' of ethnography, in its unarguable closeness to the facts of everyday school life, in what had to be its relevance to their problems.

Both groups were disappointed, although in different ways. The basis of the disappointment, most generally, was that anthropologists and sociologists remained social scientists, oriented towards their native disciplines rather than toward the discipline and institutions of education. If the people monitoring the new experiments expected anthropologists to police the experiments they were supporting, they were wrong. Anthropologists have good reason to avoid working for the established powers, having been stung on that score before.

We all know that we cannot continue to do research if we go around telling bosses that the workers are goofing or stealing. If we tell research administrators that their experiments are phony, we will not do any more research.

I'm not sure how anthropological researchers solved this problem in all the places they encountered it. It was one of the great difficulties. Even when anthropologists were quite firm in their refusal to squeal that way, guilty teachers and local administrators (who often really did have something to hide) worried that they might. If a local administrator received money for an innovation but used it to cover routine expenses and never did the experiment – who should the anthropologists tell about that? This often erupted as an argument over who would be allowed to see the anthropologists' field notes, in which the incriminating evidence likely was to be found. Administrators, concerned with running a tight ship, could not understand why they were denied relevant evidence. Social scientists remained loyal to disciplinary standards, for in the long run they would make their professional lives in social science, not in school organizations. Concerned with the long-range consequences, for themselves and the field, of letting their data be used for nonscientific purposes, they would not cooperate.

Similarly, anthropologists and sociologists were unlikely to produce 'solutions' to the problems of educators who wanted to do better. The understanding produced by our research and theory may be fine-grained and detailed enough to produce solutions, but not ones that will meet the criteria that operate in the educational setting. What I mean is this: We often can see what is causing the trouble, why some technique of teaching or administration is having an effect exactly opposite to what people want and hope for. But what we see as the cause is not something the people who look to us for help can do anything about. Or, at least, they can only do something about it at some cost so great that they are not willing to pay it.

Here is an example. When Blanche Geer, Everett Hughes, Anselm Strauss, and I produced a draft of our study of a medical school (eventually published as *Boys in White*), the doctors in that school who read it – the more thoughtful and dedicated teachers – wanted us to make recommendations. For instance, we described (apparently convincingly) how students studied for exams. Student study methods were the usual ones: cram as much factual material as you can into your head just before the test and forget it all afterward. That appalled teachers. They wanted students to take a more professional attitude toward their work. We explained to them that they provoked this sort of studying by the kind of exams they gave, which called for exactly that sort of fragmented factual knowledge. 'If you want students to study differently,' we said, 'you can do it by giving them a different kind of exam. What do you want them to know?' They wanted students to be able to make a physical examination, take a medical history, establish a diagnosis, and plan a course of treatment. Our ethnographic knowledge immediately suggested how this could be done: give each student one or two patients to examine and treat, and then let the teachers evaluate how well they had done it.

The faculty looked glum when we said that. What was wrong? That, one said, would take a lot of time, and they all had their research to attend to and their own patients to take care of. Our solution would work, of course, but it wasn't *practical*. That is the difficulty. What a social scientist identifies as a cause is usually something the people can't do anything about. So we fail the serious educational reformers on the firing line as well.

Why do we produce such useless advice? Because we are loyal to the traditions of our disciplines, which tell us that these are the kinds of answers worth having, the only kind that will work in the long run. (I believe that, but I can see that it means that practitioners are never going to be happy with the results of my research in educational institutions.)

The implication of all this is that ethnographers of education are never going to work their way out of their bad reputation. Not, at least, as long as they keep on doing good work and the schools keep failing at their job. Not as long as we come up with impractical solutions to chronic problems. Some fun!

References

Acker, S. (ed.) (1989) *Teachers, Gender and Careers*, Lewes: Falmer Press.

Astin, A.W. (1968) Undergraduate achievement and institutional excellence, *Science*, 161: 661-8.

Atkinson, P. (1981) *The Clinical Experience*, Aldershot: Gower.

Batten, T.R. (1948) *Problems of African Development*, London: Oxford University Press.

Batten, T.R. (1953) *Tropical Africa in World History*, 2nd edn London: Oxford University Press.

Becher, T. (1989) *Academic Tribes and Territories*, Milton Keynes: Open University Press.

Beck, B. and Becker, H.S. (1969) Modest proposals for graduate programs in sociology, *American Sociologist* (August): 227-34.

Becker, H.S. (1951a) The professional dance musician and his audience, *American Journal of Sociology*, 52: 136-44.

Becker, H.S. (1951b) Role and Career Problems of the Chicago Public School Teacher. PhD dissertation, University of Chicago.

Becker, H.S. (1952a) Social-class variations in the teacher pupil relationship, *Journal of Educational Sociology*, 25: 451-65.

Becker, H.S. (1952b) The career of the Chicago public schoolteacher, *American Journal of Sociology*, 52: 336-43.

Becker, H.S. (1953) The teacher in the authority system of the public school, *Journal of Educational Sociology*, 26: 128-41.

Becker, H.S. (1958) Problems of inference and proof in participant observation, *American Sociological Review*, 23: 652-60.

Becker, H.S. (1960) Notes on the concept of commitment, *American Journal of Sociology*, 66: 32-40.

Becker, H.S. (1963) *Outsiders: Studies in the Sociology of Deviance*, New York: The Free Press.

Becker, H.S. (1964) Personal change in adult life, *Sociometry*, 27: 40-53. Also in Becker, H.S. (1970), *Sociological Work*, Chicago: Aldine.

Becker, H.S. (1966) Introduction [to *The Jack Roller*], in C. Shaw, *The Jack Roller*, 2nd edn Chicago: University of Chicago Press.

Becker, H.S. (1967) History, culture and subjective experience: an exploration of the social bases of drug-induced experiences, *Journal of Health and Social Behaviour*, 14: 239-47.

Becker, H.S. (1970) *Sociological Work*, Chicago: Aldine.

Becker, H.S. (1971) Comment, in M. Wax, S. Diamond and F.O. Gearing (eds) *Anthropological Perspectives on Education*, New York: Basic Books, p. 10.

Becker, H.S. (1983) Art worlds and social types, *Sociologie du Travail*, 83 (4): 404–17.

Becker, H.S. (1986) *Writing for Social Scientists*, Chicago: University of Chicago Press.

Becker, H.S. (1992) Cases, causes, conjunctures, stories and imagery', in C.C. Ragin and H.S. Becker (eds) *What is a Case? Exploring the Foundations of Social Inquiry*, Cambridge: Cambridge University Press, pp. 205–16.

Becker, H.S. and Strauss, A.L. (1956) Careers, personality and adult socialisation, *American Journal of Sociology*, 62: 253–63.

Becker, H.S. and Geer, B. (1958) The fate of idealism in medical school, *American Sociological Review*, 23: 50–6.

Becker, H.S. and Geer, B. (1960a) Latent culture: a note on the theory of latent social roles, *Administrative Science Quarterly*, 5: 304–13.

Becker, H.S. and Geer, B. (1960b) Participant observation: the analysis of qualitative field data, in R.N. Adams and J.J. Preiss (eds) *Human Organisation Research*, Homewood, Illinois: Dorsey Press, pp. 267–89.

Becker, H.S., Geer, B., Strauss, A.L. and Hughes, E.C. (1961) *Boys in White: Student Culture in Medical School*, Chicago: University of Chicago Press.

Becker, H.S., Geer, B. and Hughes, E.C. (1968) *Making the Grade: The Academic Side of College Life*, New York: John Wiley.

Blumer, H. (1939) *Critiques of Research in the Social Sciences: An Appraisal of Thomas and Znaniecki's 'The Polish Peasant in Europe and America'*, New York: Social Science Research Council.

Blumer, H. (1966) 'Sociological implications of the thought of George Herbert Mead, *American Journal of Sociology*, 71: 535–44.

Blumer, H. (1969) *Symbolic Interactionism: Perspective or Method*, Englewood Cliffs, New Jersey: Prentice Hall.

Brim, O.G. (1960) Personality as role learning, in I. Iscoe and H. Stevenson (eds) *Personality Development in Children*, Austin: University of Texas Press, pp. 127–59.

Brim, O.G. and Wheeler, S. (1966) *Socialisation after Childhood*, New York: John Wiley.

Bryman, A. and Burgess, R.G. (eds) (1994) *Analysing Qualitative Data*, London: Routledge.

Burgess, R.G. (1983) *Experiencing Comprehensive Education: A Study of Bishop McGregor School*, London: Methuen.

Burgess, R.G. (1984a) *In the Field: An Introduction to Field Research*, London: Allen and Unwin.

Burgess, R.G. (1984b) Exploring frontiers and settling territory: shaping the sociology of education, *British Journal of Sociology*, 35(1): 122–37.

Burgess, R.G. (1986) *Sociology, Education and Schools: An Introduction to the Sociology of Education*, London: Batsford.

Burgess, R.G. (1993) Event analysis and the study of headship, in M. Schratz (ed.) *Qualitative Voices*, Lewes: Falmer Press.

Burgess, R.G. and Rudduck, J. (eds) (1993) *A Perspective on Educational Case Study: A Collection of Papers by Lawrence Stenhouse*, University of Warwick: CEDAR.

Christie, R. and Merton, R.K. (1958) Procedures for the sociological study of the values climate of medical school, *Journal of Medical Education*, 33(2): 125–53.

Cloward, R.A. and Ohlin, L.E. (1960) *Delinquency and Opportunity: A Theory of Delinquent Gangs*, New York: The Free Press.

Cloward, R.A. *et al.* (1960) *Theoretical Studies in Social Organisation of the Prison*, New York: Social Science Research Council.

Clute, K.F. (1963) *The General Practitioner: A Study of Medical Education and Practice in Ontario and Nova Scotia*, Toronto: University of Toronto Press.

Cockburn, J. (1984) The Use of Interviewing in Social Science Research with Special Reference to Education. PhD thesis, University of East Anglia.

Cohen, A.K. (1955) *Delinquent Boys: The Culture of a Gang*, New York: The Free Press.

Cooley, C.H. (1902) *Human Nature and the Social Order*, New York: Charles Scribner.

Cooley, C.H. (1927) *Social Organisation*, New York: Charles Scribner.

Cressey, D.R. (ed.) (1961) *The Prison: Studies in Institutional Organisation and Change*, New York: Holt, Rinehart and Winston.

Cunningham, J.R. (1941) Education, in L.S.S. O'Maley (ed.) *Modern India and the West*, London: Oxford University Press.

Dalton, M. (1951) Informal factors in career achievement, *American Journal of Sociology*, 56: 407–15.

Davis, A. (1946) The motivation of the underprivileged worker, in W.F. Whyte (ed.) *Industry and Society*, New York: McGraw Hill.

Davis, A. (1950) *Social Class Influences Upon Learning*, Cambridge: Harvard University Press.

Davis, F. and Olesen, V.L. (1963) Initiation into a women's profession, *Sociometry*, 26: 89–101.

Delamont, S. (1981) 'All too familiar? A decade of classroom research, *Educational Analysis*, 3(1): 69–83.

Delamont, S. (1983) *Interaction in the Classroom*, 2nd edn London: Methuen.

Denzin, N. (1992) *Symbolic Interactionism and Cultural Studies*, Oxford: Blackwell.

Dewey, J. (1930) *Human Nature and Conduct*, New York: Holt, Rinehart and Winston.

Eells, K. *et al.* (1951) *Intelligence and Cultural Differences*, Chicago: University of Chicago Press.

Eron, L.D. (1955) Effect of medical education on medical students, *Journal of Medical Education*, 10: 559–66.

Fielding, N.G. and Lee, R.M. (eds) (1991) *Using Computers in Qualitative Research*, London: Sage.

Forsyth, S. and Kolenda, P.M. (1966) Competition, co-operation and group cohesion in the ballet company, *Psychiatry*, 29: 123–45.

Friedson, E. (1961) *Patients' Views of Medical Practice*, New York: Russell Sage Foundation.

Friedson, E. (1970) *The Profession of Medicine*, New York: Dodd Mead.

Geer, B. (1966) Occupational commitment and the teaching profession, *The School Review*, 74(1): 31–47.

Geer, B. (1968) Teaching, *International Encyclopedia of the Social Sciences*, New York: Macmillan and The Free Press, 560–5.

Gerth, H.H. and Mills, C.W. (1946) *From Max Weber: Essays in Sociology*, New York: Oxford University Press.

Goffman, E. (1961) *Asylums: Essays on the Social Situation of Mental Patients and Other Inmates*, Garden City: Doubleday.

Goodman, P. (1968) Mini-schools: a prescription for the reading problem, *New York Review of Books*, 9: 16–18.

Hall, O. (1948) The stages of a medical career, *American Journal of Sociology*, 53: 327–36.

Hall, O. (1949) Types of medical careers, *American Journal of Sociology*, 55: 243–53.

Hammersley, M. (1989) *The Dilemma of Qualitative Method*, London: Routledge.

Hammersley, M. and Atkinson, P. (1983) *Ethnography: Principles into Practice*, London: Tavistock.

Hargreaves, A. (1986) *The Two Cultures of Schooling: The Case of Middle Schools*, Lewes: Falmer Press.

Herndon, J. (1968) *The Way it was Spozed to Be*, New York: Bantam.

Hoffman, T. (n.d.) The Acting Student: Species, Habitat, Behaviour, unpublished.

Hollingshead, A. (1949) *Elmtown's Youth*, New York: John Wiley.

Holt, J. (1967) *How Children Learn*, New York: Pitman.

Hughes, E.C. (1937) Institutional office and the person, *American Journal of Sociology*, 42: 404–13.

Hughes, E.C. (1942) The study of institutions, *Social Forces*, 20: 307–10.

Hughes, E.C. (1943) *French Canada in Transition*, Chicago: University of Chicago Press.

Hughes, E.C. (1951) Studying the nurse's work, *American Journal of Nursing* (May): 294–5.

Hughes, E.C. (1952) *Where Peoples Meet*, Glencoe: The Free Press.

Hughes, E.C. (1958) *Men and their Work*, New York: The Free Press.

Irwin, J. and Cressey, D.R. (1962) Thieves, convicts and the inmate culture, *Social Problems*, 10 (Fall): 142–55.

Jacob, P. (1957) *Changing Values in College: An Exploratory Study of the Impact of College Teaching*, New York: Harper.

Kuhn, M. (1964) Major trends in symbolic interaction theory in the past twenty five years, *Sociological Quarterly*, 5: 61–84.

Lacey, C. (1977) *The Socialization of Teachers*, London: Methuen.

Leyburn, J.G. (1941) *The Haitian People*, New Haven: Yale University Press.

Lindesmith, A.R. (1947) *Opiate Addiction*, Bloomington, Indiana: Principia Press.

MacDowell, H. (1954) The Principal's Role in a Metropolitan School System, PhD thesis, University of Chicago.

Maunier, R. (1949) *The Sociology of Colonies*, E.O. Lorimer (ed./transl.), London: Routledge.

Mayhew, A. (1926) *The Education of India*, London: Faber and Gwyer.

McCall, G.J. and Simmons, J.L. (1966) *Identities and Interactions*, New York: The Free Press.

Mead, G.H. (1934) *Mind, Self and Society*, Chicago: University of Chicago Press.

Mechanic, D. (1962) *Students Under Street*, New York: The Free Press.

Merton, R.K., Kendall, P. and Reader, G. (1957) (eds) *The Student Physician*, Cambridge, Massachusetts: Harvard University Press.

Miller, S.J. (1970) *Prescription for Excellence*, Chicago: Aldine.

Nuffield Foundation and the Colonial Office (1953) *African Education: A Study of Educational Policy and Practice in British Tropical Africa*, Oxford: Oxford University Press.

Peterson, O.L., Andrews, L.P., Spain, R.S. and Greenberg, B.G. (1956) An analytical study of North Carolina general practice 1953–1954, *Journal of Medical Education*, 31: 1–165.

Pollard, A. (1985) *The Social World of the Primary School*, London: Holt, Rinehart and Winston.

Powney, J. and Watts, M. (1987) *Interviewing in Educational Research*, London: Routledge.

Rock, P. (1979) *The Making of Symbolic Interactionism*, London: Methuen.

Roy, D. (1952) Quota restriction and goldbricking in a machine shop, *American Journal of Sociology*, 53: 427–42.

Schatzman, L. and Strauss, A. (1955) Social class and modes of communication, *American Journal of Sociology*, 60: 329–38.

Selznick, P. (1953) *TVA and the Grass Roots*, Berkeley, California: University of California Press.

Shaw, C. (1930) *The Jack Roller*, Chicago: University of Chicago Press.

Smith, M.G. (1953) Social structure in the British Caribbean about 1820, *Social and Economic Studies*, 1(4): 55–79.

Smith, M.G. (1954) Slavery and emancipation in two societies, *Social and Economic Studies*, 3(3) and 4: 239–90.

Sparkes, A.C. (1988) The micropolitics of innovation in the physical education curriculum, in J. Evans (ed.) *Teachers, Teaching and Control in Physical Education*, Lewes: Falmer Press, pp. 157–77.

Spindler, G. (1982) (ed.) *Doing the Ethnography of Schooling: Educational Anthropology in Action*, New York: Holt, Rinehart and Winston.

Spindler, G. and Spindler, L. (1982) Roger Harker and Schönhausen: from the familiar to the strange and back again, in G. Spindler (ed.) *Doing the Ethnography of Schooling: Educational Anthropology in Action*, New York: Holt, Rinehart and Winston, pp. 20-46.

Stanton, A. and Schwartz, M. (1954) *The Mental Hospital*, New York: Basic Books.

Strauss, A.L. (1952) The development and transformation of many meanings in the child, *American Sociological Review*, 17: 275–86.

Strauss, A.L. (1959) *Mirrors and Masks: The Search for Identity*, New York: The Free Press.

Sumner, W.G. (1907) *Folkways*, Boston: Ginn.

Tax, S. (1946) The education of underprivileged peoples in dependent and independent territories, *Journal of Negro Education*, 15: 336–45.

Thomas, W.I. and Znaniecki, F. (1918–20) *The Polish Peasant in Europe and America*, Chicago: University of Chicago Press.

Tugwell, R.G. (1947) *The Stricken Land*, New York: Doubleday.

van der Kroef, J.M. (1954) Educational development and social change in Indonesia, *Harvard Educational Review*, 24 (Fall): 239–55.

Verhoeven, J. (1989) *Methodological and Metascientific Problems in Symbolic Interactionism*, Leuven: Department of Sociology, Katholieke Universiteit Leuven, Belgium.

Wagenschein, M. (1950) Reality Shock, MA thesis, University of Chicago.

Waller, W. (1932) *Sociology of Teaching*, New York: John Wiley.

Warner, W.L., Havighurst, R.J. and Loeb, M.B. (1944) *Who Shall be Educated?*, New York: Routledge.

Warner, W.L. and Lunt, P. (1941) *The Social Life of a Modern Community*, New Haven: Yale University Press.

Wheeler, S. (1961) Socialisation in correctional communities, *American Sociological Review*, 26: 697–712.

Winget, J. (1952) Teacher Interschool Mobility Aspirations: Elementary Teachers, Chicago Public School System, 1947–48. PhD dissertation, University of Chicago.

Wolff, K. (1950) *The Sociology of Georg Simmel* (transl.), Glencoe: The Free Press, p. 235.

Woods, P. (1979) *The Divided School*, London: Routledge and Kegan Paul.

Woods, P. (1980) (ed.) *Teacher Strategies: Explorations in the Sociology of the School*, London: Croom Helm.

Woods, P. (1983) *Sociology and the School: An Interactionist Viewpoint*, London: Routledge and Kegan Paul.

Woods, P. (1990) *The Happiest Days? How Pupils Cope with School*, Lewes: Falmer Press.

Woods, P. (1991) *Teachers' Skills and Strategies*, Lewes: Falmer Press.

Name Index

Subject Index

GENDERED EDUCATION

Sandra Acker

Sandra Acker explores fundamental themes in the study of women and education. With arguments grounded in sound scholarship and empirical evidence, and a style that is clear and accessible without minimizing the complexities behind the issues, she addresses invisibilities and inequities in the sociology of education, the careers of women teachers and the experiences of women academics. She examines the development of the sociology of women's education, assesses the contributions of feminist theory and feminist research to educational enquiry, and considers whether gender equity in education is nearly with us or still a feminist fantasy. Sandra Acker is interested in understanding when work settings facilitate or limit scholarship, beliefs and careers; why feminism is resisted by teachers and education policy-makers; and how gender can be made central to scholarship.

Contents

208pp   0 335 19059 6 (Paperback)   0 335 19060 X (Hardback)

STUDYING CURRICULUM
CASES AND METHODS

Ivor F. Goodson

Studying Curriculum offers a fruitful and practical approach for analysing the inescapable political realities of the contemporary curriculum. It reminds us that what is socially constructed can also be deconstructed and reconstructed, and that notions of social equity and justice can be reconstituted within school curricula. As Andy Hargreaves notes in his critical introduction to this volume: 'such a combination of conceptual and political radicalism, and empirical and historical realism not only defines Goodson's scholarship but also demystifies the curriculum it addresses'.

Ivor Goodson explores how and by whom the curriculum is controlled. He examines how social background and origin, historical and political context, and school curriculum are interrelated. He takes a social constructionist approach, and plants this firmly in the 'middle ground' of subjects – their traditions, departments and politics. This enables both a rendering of the experience of those working within these traditions; and a reaching outwards to the structures and assumptions underlying those subject traditions.

Contents

160pp   0 335 19050 2 (Paperback)   0 335 19051 0 (Hardback)

RACISM AND EDUCATION
RESEARCH PERSPECTIVES
Barry Troyna

The dilemma facing educational systems in culturally diverse societies is both real and demanding. Too much allowance for diversity can lead to fragmentation and loss of control; too little, to alienation, unrest and loss of control.

Over the past decade or so, Barry Troyna has been involved actively in research aimed at illuminating the role played by educational policy and provision in the legitimation and reproduction of racial inequalities. In the first part of *Racism and Education: Research Perspectives* he draws on his research into educational policy at both state and institutional level to argue that policy makers and practitioners have avoided getting to grips with one of the central impulses of culturally and ethnically mixed societies: racism.

In the second part he focuses on the research enterprise itself. He highlights some of the methodological limitations of existing research on multicultural and antiracist education – research, that is, which has played a powerful role in the framing of educational policy and practice. In the final chapter of the book Troyna provides a vigorous and provocative defence of antiracist education against the criticisms mounted by those of the New Right, multiculturalists and 'critical revisionists'.

Contents

176pp   0 335 15778 5 (Paperback)   0 335 15779 3 (Hardback)